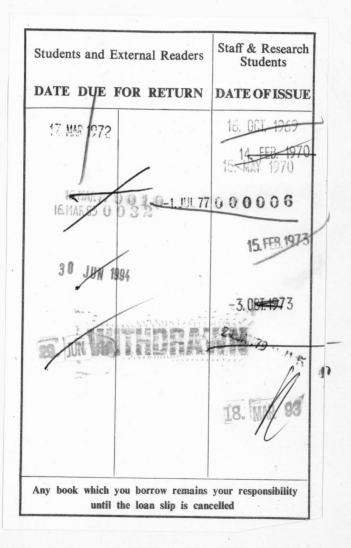

Students and External Readers	Staff & Research Students
DATE DUE FOR RETURN	**DATE OF ISSUE**
17 MAR 1972	16. OCT. 1969
	14. FEB. 1970
	15. MAY 1970
16. MAR	-1. JUL. 77 0 0 0 0 0 6
	15. FEB. 1973
30 JUN 1994	
	-3. OCT. 1973
WITHDRAWN	
	18. MAY 93

Any book which you borrow remains your responsibility until the loan slip is cancelled

SOCIOLOGY, THEOLOGY AND CONFLICT

PAPERS BY

M. BROADY   A. E. HILLS

H. COMPTON   J. KLEIN

F. W. DILLISTONE   R. MARTIN

M. C. GOLDSMITH   B. BABINGTON SMITH

D. E. H. WHITELEY

SOCIOLOGY, THEOLOGY AND CONFLICT

Edited by

D. E. H. WHITELEY

and

R. MARTIN

BASIL BLACKWELL
OXFORD
1969

631 12150 1

PRINTED IN GREAT BRITAIN
BY A. T. BROOME AND SON, 18 ST. CLEMENT'S, OXFORD
AND BOUND BY THE KEMP HALL BINDERY, OXFORD

CONTENTS

EDITORS' NOTE

Individual contributions represent the views of the individual author, not of the group as a whole or of the editors. The editors have refrained from making any alterations to the text of particular essays, even where they may disagree with the views expressed.

INTRODUCTION

This book is intended for those who are capable of reading 'Pelicans', and who are interested in at least some of its contents: it is not intended for the professional academic. The initiative in having it written was taken by the Council of the Modern Churchmen's Union which defrayed the cost of getting the papers duplicated and of the small conference at which they were discussed. The book is in some respects a successor to *Biology* and *Personality*, edited by Professor Ian T. Ramsey, of Oriel College, Oxford, and now Bishop of Durham, which was also sponsored by the Modern Churchmen's Union, and published by Basil Blackwell in 1965.

There are, however, two important differences between the present work and *Biology and Personality*. First, the earlier book consisted of a series of chapters in which recent advances in factual knowledge within the sphere of the biological sciences were expounded, and their interpretation discussed. In addition, their bearing upon theological and moral issues was considered. The lack of agreement about the concepts used in interpreting social behaviour inevitably meant that more time was spent during the conference in discussing concepts and ideas than in exchanging new information. This emphasis is reflected in the present volume, whose contribution lies less in imparting new facts than in discussing the concepts used in sociology and theology respectively. It is hoped that the exchange will lead to cross-fertilization. Theology has already gained from an awareness of the problems studied by sociologists. I well remember a point made by the late Henry McGowan, then an Archdeacon in Birmingham and subsequently Bishop of Wakefield. He said that a clergyman who was about to be consecrated Bishop should first be taken to a typical factory and addressed in the following terms: 'A quarter of the men working in this plant were confirmed by a Bishop like you are going to be. Now talk with them, and see if you can tell which have been confirmed and which have not'. In other words, no theologian should make any statement about the relation between membership of the Church, or the sacraments on the one hand and moral conduct on the other, or indeed any *factual*

1

statement, unless it has been factually tested and proved to be correct. Similarly, many non-Christians are somewhat naive about theology, supposing theological language to be factual when in reality it might better be described as 'poetry plus'. In confrontations between Christians and non-Christians, and indeed between Christians of opposing views, it is essential to be clear about the language 'wave-length', about whether language is intended to convey factual information, and if not, just what function it is intended to perform.

The first respect then, in which the present book differs from *Biology and Personality* is that the emphasis is less upon newly discovered facts than upon concepts and interpretation. The second difference is that the earlier book included the discussion which followed each paper while in the present work another procedure has been adopted. The contributions had been duplicated and circulated beforehand, and lively discussion resulted. This discussion has not been recorded, since it proved difficult to discern—or manufacture—a clear line of argument. Instead, some of the papers were altered in the light of the discussions to avoid misunderstanding, and many of the points raised have been noted in this introduction.

The contributors to this volume are sociologists and theologians. Broady, Klein, and Martin are all academic sociologists, teaching and researching in universities. Babington Smith holds a similar post in psychology. Dillistone and I have the same university duties in theology, in addition to pastoral responsibility for students. Hills is engaged in theological research. Goldsmith has had a theological training and has pastoral duties towards the students of the University of Aston in Birmingham. Compton formerly taught at what is now the University of Aston and is at present a free-lance business adviser and journalist. Some of us are Christians and some are not. Readers are invited to see whether they can infer from the papers which contributors are in fact Christian. Dr. Gough, a psychiatrist, also attended and took part in the discussion, as did the Rev. E. Compton, the Rev. C. Rhodes, and the Rev. H. C. Snape.

We deliberately avoided asking Roman Catholics on the ground that in a short conference where it is hoped to generate constructive clashes of opinion it is unwise to mix too many different types. We also excluded representatives of the 'Christendom' group, who already have well-articulated views on the relation between Theology and Sociology.

As academics we may all seem to belong to the world of the ivory tower, set apart from the interests of the 'ordinary man'. However, as teachers we are made only too aware of the problems of the 'real' world by our students, young men and women all involved in the difficulties of growing to maturity in the 'real' world. In any case, academic life is just as 'real' as the life of a bus conductor. We all of us, whether professional men, clerks, fitters, process workers or teachers in universities, live in towers of our own, and our horizons are limited by the demands of our occupation. Yet, at the same time, we share common concerns and can learn from each other.

It may seem strange to bring out a book about sociology just when there are some signs that the subject is beginning to lose its magical appeal. Only last summer a sociology student at a university justly renowned in this subject said to the Professor of Sociology: 'You have wasted three years of my life!' The false glamour of sociology is beginning to wear off, and there is a danger that the modest but real value of sociology when practised by sober-minded and competent scholars may be disregarded because of the way in which it had been over-sold. It has been recently said of sociology as it was said of psychology in the 1930's, that it is 'an unholy mixture of common sense and uncommon nonsense'. It should be said at once that much nonsense has been talked by the theologians, sociologists, psychologists—and scientists! But it is pure prejudice to condemn a subject because of exaggerated expectations. It is not surprising that a genuine academic study often gives support to what we say we know by common sense. Argyle has shown that those who are active members of some religious group have a higher standard of moral behaviour, as measured by crude indicators like convictions in the law courts. To some this finding will seem 'only what one would expect': to others it would appear surprising or even a disappointment. Again, most of us would take the 'common sense' view that the more contented workers are, the more they will produce. But, as Compton points out (p. 164), a measure of discontent does in fact, appear to lead to *higher* productivity. It would be wilful stupidity to disregard what sociologists can tell us about some of the problems which are likely to cause trouble in the future. How are we to face the difficulty of less employment in factories caused by automation? Many clerks may suffer redundancy and relative loss of status through the introduction of computers. Sociologists have no magic power to overcome these troubles, but they can at least warn us what to expect and give us the benefit of an informed opinion.

The facts collected by those who study the sociology of religion confirm the impression gathered over the years by the 'plain man' and place in sharper focus the theological riddles which they raise. For example, it has often been popularly imagined that salvation is limited to those whom God has predestined to be members of the Church. This view is rarely held by theologians or by instructed Church or Chapel goers, but it survives as a kind of folk-memory among those whose great-grandparents drifted out of the Church in the last century. Now social surveys of religious practice and affiliation have made it clear that in Britain and the USA affiliation to Christian bodies is characteristic of income groups which are mainly found in the suburbs, and not character-istic of those who live in the 'burnt-out city-centre' or in the new housing estates. Are we to say: 'God so loved the suburbs that . . . .?' This would be straight blasphemy. It is clear then that any person who has an interest in religion should be familiar with the relevant facts laid bare by the sociologists.

But can we maintain that those interested in the problems studied by sociologists, whether they themselves are professional sociologists or intelligent members of the general public, should also pay attention to religion? Two classes of men will obviously do so: first, those who on other grounds believe that religion is 'true' or rather, since no instructed Christian or, I imagine, any adherent of other religions, is so naive as to suppose that he has got the truth neatly tied up, those who believe that religion is a valid approach to reality even though, as St. Paul said over nineteen centuries ago, 'We see only puzzling reflections in a mirror' (I Corinthians, xiii, 12, *N.E.B.*); and secondly, those who are themselves agnostics but devote their professional expertise to research in the Sociology of Religion. I believe, however, that an awareness of religion and of theology, quite independently of whether Christianity or any other religion is 'true', can be of value to a far wider circle. Firstly, there is an overlap of subject matter between theology and the social sciences: both are concerned with human behaviour and human welfare. Both analyse this overlap of subject matter in different ways, and can therefore be expected to give help to each other.

Secondly, religious people, by which phrase I here refer to those whose lives are dominated by religion, find personal satisfaction and a sense of purpose for themselves and for the world through this religion. If religion is in any sense true, so that the adherents of, e.g., Christianity, find satisfaction and a sense of purpose through something which is 'true' though inevitably expressed to a large extent in 'picture language', then this religion is worthy of the closest investigation. But if all religions are basically fairy tales and owe their appeal mainly to wishful thinking, even then the fact that people do find various religious 'fairy stories' satisfying does at least tell us something about the emotional and other needs of those people. If we knew more about what it was that made religion such a force in certain sections of Victorian England and Wales it might be possible to fill this emotional need, preferably with something 'true', instead of leaving a mere void. I suggest this on the assumption that religion is in no sense true. It is only honest to say that I do not personally share this assumption, and that in my own view most human beings, if not all, have a need, conscious or unconscious, which can ultimately be met only by religion. I am not saying that the Victorians knew the truth and that we should return to it. Religion is certainly not 'true' in the same sense as the natural sciences. Though both science and religion make use of 'models' or picture language, religion does so to a far greater extent. Nor do I suggest that the 'picture language' of a past age is necessarily suitable for today. Different 'pictures' assist different people towards an appreciation of realities which can not be described in 'literal' terms. (Those familiar with theology will be puzzled that I should have spent time on the commonplace platitudes expressed in the last few lines. The reason is that for those whose interest is not theology but sociology they may not be platitudes at all, but genuinely unfamiliar. It may even be imagined that I am pushing an individual line of my own. In fact, I have merely been expressing in my own words what official theology has for many centuries called the Doctrine of Analogy.)

So far I have tried to explain why this conference was held and why the duplicated papers discussed there have been published. It must now be said that as the discussions proceeded, engendering heat of various degrees, we were all progressively aware of the fact that we were returning again and again to a single problem: the problem of alienation.

It is clear that 'alienation' is a single word which is applied to a number of different phenomena. It is discussed later (pp. 29ff.), but for the present it may be said that we use the word alienation when an 'us and them' situation develops. We use it especially when each side acquires a 'stereotyped' view of the other, and is unwilling to accept evidence in its favour. We use 'alienation' also when communication between the two groups becomes more difficult and when the dispute 'escalates'.

It is tempting in this century of wars to imagine that we ought to aim at a state of affairs in which there is no rivalry and no conflict. We are rescued from this natural temptation both by a shrewd suspicion that a condition like this cannot be attained and by an awareness of the teaching of theology. What do we mean, for example, by the 'sinlessness of Christ'? In this connection, Professor John Macquarrie (*Principles of Christian Theology*, first British edition, London 1966, p. 277) says: 'We must consider sinlessness as the end of a process of development. . . . Thus 'sinlessness' means that the disorder is overcome, and . . . is gained in the needs and decisions of life, and is, certainly not a merely negative 'dreaming innocence'. This means that, according to the Christian belief in the 'sinlessness of Jesus', Our Lord was not free from infant tantrums, but lived through them and integrated his 'infantile' aggression into a balanced personality. It should be made clear for the benefit of non-theologians that Macquarrie is not a way-out left wing writer, but a responsible and sober spokesman of generally accepted contemporary theology. This suggests that conflict is not something which should be banished, but lived through in order that alienation may be prevented. This conclusion that strife should be lived through and not merely suppressed is also in line with my own theological presupposition that: 'God's purpose for human beings living on this planet is that they should live together, strive against each other and with their environment and so develop into beings capable of loving God and each other', (p. 70).

This opinion about the necessity for some degree of conflict was expressed by the writers of papers and arose spontaneously in discussions. It is not that we tamely accepted each other's opinions —we were not that sort of conference! It is rather that the same realization was borne in upon all of us by the sheer facts of the case. The point was raised most trenchantly by the Rev. Malcolm Goldsmith, Chaplain to the University of Aston, who, in the course of a paper devoted to showing how the ordinary person can avoid being 'pushed around' by 'them', said that wild-cat strikes, simply because they involve defiance both of management and of the union officials, give a great boost to the morale of the strikers, and enable them to feel that they are still human beings in spite of the fact that under normal conditions they are minute cogs in a vast system of economic machinery (p. 48). He roundly declared that: 'It is very doubtful whether the moves by certain influential people to make unofficial strikes illegal is a progressive step at all.'

Like other members of the group I am personally unable to share his opinion. In an economic system as complex and as interdependent as our own, where the withdrawal from work of a few key men can reduce thousands to idleness, a point does come where the few ought not to assert their human dignity in a way which does disproportionate harm to others. It is easy to sneer at merely economic loss, which Mr. Goldsmith was far too sensible to do. Loss of production does not merely harm dividends: it leads to hunger here and starvation in the developing countries. At the level of human dignity, wildcat strikers may cause their fellow workers to be deprived of the dignity of doing a job. All of us, when 'asserting' our dignity, should be careful to avoid affronting the dignity of other people.

But it would be inexcusably superficial to dismiss this particular contention by Mr. Goldsmith as I have so far done. I think he has gone too far in the matter of unofficial strikes. I do not propose to draw the line myself. After all, I am an academic theologian, and I have not the knowledge to speak about industry. But the supremely important principle he has raised is that all our economic systems exist for the sake of human beings, and not the other way round. Dr. Broady makes the same essential point in his paper on 'Higher Education in a Technological Society'. The economic system and the educational system which is so dangerously dependent upon it exist for the sake of human beings and not *vice versa*.

This is basically in line with some fundamental propositions of Theology. 'The Sabbath was made for the sake of man and not man for the Sabbath', are the words ascribed to Jesus in Mark ii. 27 (*New English Bible*). The Sabbath was perhaps the greatest of all institutions to the Jew, so for Christians there is no institution which does not exist for the sake of man. It may be said that the doctrine of the supremacy of man over institutions is not peculiar to Christians: humanists also accept it. But in a case like this we should unite to put a principle into practice, not squabble about patent rights. It may be said also that this principle is a platitude. Quite right. It *is* a platitude, but because we have so signally failed to apply it we must consider it an *important* platitude.

Granted then that systems exist for the sake of man, we must return to a consideration of human needs. In order to grow and develop human beings must be given opportunities of interaction, as Dr. Klein points out (p. 134). I hasten to add that I do not accept her specific proposal for hostels where sexual experimentation is permitted, but her main contention that personal interaction, quite apart from sex, is necessary for maturity, remains unshaken. This interaction may escalate into conflict. This does not apply at the personal, individual level alone: groups, as well as individuals, need to 'confront' each other, and serious conflict may arise, nuclear war being to date the gravest possibility. Dr. Martin reminds us that in the United States there is: 'a loss of community which only some form of communal identification wider than the nuclear family yet smaller than society as a whole can provide'. Conflict is liable to develop between these groups also. We see signs of this conflict in Welsh and Scottish Nationalism and in the tension between French and Flemish speaking Belgians.

We must note in passing an even graver difficulty. For emotional health we need to identify with something smaller than the nation state. But economic health requires planning to be carried out on a larger scale than that of the individual state. Indeed, we all know in our hearts that not only economic planning but population planning as well (I only hope that compulsion will be avoided) must be effected on a world scale. But this problem raises hope. In recent years the nation state has been the unit both of patriotic identification and of economic planning: it is now in many cases too large for the first and too small for the second.

For myself, I 'identify' most passionately with the United Kingdom. But I believe that in the next millennium or even sooner we must have our chief communal identifications at different levels from our economic organization. Perhaps in future a Welshman will identify primarily with Wales and secondarily with the U.K., while economic policy is decided on a worldwide basis.

The last paragraph was an aside. We return to the problem created by the fact that confrontation of individual with individual and of group with group is essential for growth and maturity, while these necessary confrontations may give rise to unspeakable holocausts. We need not a rigid system, but a developing system in a state of dynamic tension which is capable of 'containing' opposition and even conflict in order to forestall disaster in the shape of nuclear war or any other form.

At a very elementary level we can view the human body as an example of a system of checks and balances. If we get too cold we shiver and the heat generated by this activity helps to restore the balance. If we get too hot, then our sweat glands come into operation. But in the potentially fatal condition known as heat-stroke the cooling mechanism is overpowered with catastrophic results. Some opposition, even if it amounts to conflict, as we have already seen, is essential and may prevent the chronic condition known as alienation, that is, a long-standing them-and-us condition, from arising.

Since alienation is a portmanteau word covering a large number of conditions, and since 'malignant', as opposed to 'healthy' conflict can also take many forms, we must not take it for granted that there is a single solution.

Dr. Dillistone claims that to begin the process of overcoming alienation and so reducing potentially dangerous conflict we need 'free flow between two centres of personal life', and 'an image of wholeness' (p. 83). He goes on to say that in Christianity, especially as expounded by Paul Tillich, we find the 'free flow' in the realization that we are accepted by God, while the 'image of wholeness' is provided when 'in the New Testament picture of the Christ we are given an image of the New Reality' (p. 84). Two comments must be made, and with both of them Dr. Dillistone would be in full agreement. First, a man's religion, in the narrow sense of the word, may be the centre of his life, but it is not the

B

whole of it. A Christian, like other men, grows and matures (in the technical language of theology this is called 'sanctification') through the dynamic process of living, of reacting with other people and growing through opposition which may sometimes amount to conflict. Secondly, most people in the world are not Christians, and many of those who are adherents of some religion, including Christianity, have only the husk of customary observance and lack the kernel of dynamic involvement. It follows that for most people other means are necessary to overcome alienation and prevent conflict from reaching pathological limits.

Dr. Dillistone mentions art as an activity which helps to overcome alienation, frustration and dangerous conflict and to restore wholeness (pp. 85f). He seems to have in mind primarily art as a 'spectator' activity, that is, he seems to be concerned with the appreciation of art. This is useful for a minority, and the fact that it helps only a small minority should not lead us to despise it. Similar help is given by such activities as sport, crafts, amateur dramatics, etc. All these are of value, but merely to catalogue them, even if we include gardening, fishing and 'do it yourself' activities is to make clear the fact that useful though they may be as harmless outlets, these blameless bourgeois pastimes are wholly inadequate as a solution. Any member of an estranged group who read this paragraph would grind his teeth in rage, and feel insulted by the mention of such trivialities in connection with his trouble and I do not blame him.

Since the end of World War II we have been living on borrowed time in the sense that nuclear devastation of the entire planet has always been possible. We are still living on borrowed time, and we do not know how much time we have been lent. In addition, within each nation state there has insidiously grown in the last few years a state of violence between those of different races, languages, age groups, and occupations. It would seem that the rule of law, painfully built up over many centuries, could be lost in the remaining years of the present millenium. To shout and protest is easy. To work, cooperate and improve matters is a slower task which does not give such rapid apparent results. However, among the 'alienated' and, at least in their own view, oppressed minorities, there is a vital distinction between the sane majority who protest because they have a grievance and are prepared to work with the 'enemy' to set it right, and the dangerous minority who look for a grievance because they want to protest, and use their fellow protesters as demonstration-fodder to satisfy their own paranoia. It must be added that pathological conditions, such as paranoia, are not confined to protesters, but are found also among the 'establishment figures' against whom protests are launched.

The reason why leisure and sporting activities seem inadequate alleviations of alienation and conflict is that they are concerned only with spare-time activities and do not therefore give an adequate sense of purpose. Can sociological enquiry tell us anything about the extent to which spare-time activities are, in fact, able to overcome alienation and drain off aggression? Such an enquiry might shed light on the question whether and to what extent it may be necessary to modify industry, with a possible slowing-down of the growth of the gross national product and of the standard of living.

Again, those of us who were old enough in World War II remember that there was a certain decrease in the alienation between social and economic classes in Britain. Groups who might be partially alienated are drawn together by common opposition to the governments of South Africa and Rhodesia. This is to some extent a result of positive concern for the Africans living in the territories concerned, but it is also true that Ian Smith and others are serving a cathartic purpose for British liberals by acting as a hatred-conductor. Can sociologists tell us whether it is possible for alienation to be overcome by any force which does not involve hatred of some third group, in which case the alienation and conflict are not overcome but merely transferred? Within branches of the Christian Church, to what extent is there real brotherhood and overcoming of alienation without 'hatred' of the unconverted, normally projected upon God, or a withdrawal from 'the world' which constitutes alienation along a new line of cleavage? We should welcome whatever help can be given to us through the application of sociological techniques of enquiry in answering these and similar questions.

A brief account must be given of the papers printed in this volume which have not already received sufficient mention. Dr. Martin's 'Sociology and Theology' will tell teachers of the subject nothing new, but they will find it useful as an aid for their pupils. About many so-called introductions to sociology it has been remarked that they provide excellent revision courses for those already familiar with the subject, but contain too many technical terms introduced too quickly for the pupil to make them part of his mental framework before going on to the next chapter, which is not comprehensible unless the concepts treated in the previous chapter have been so assimilated. Dr. Martin's paper can be understood by an intelligent person at a first reading and yet conveys much valuable information.

Dr. Broady in his first paper contends that the Church ought not to 'go it alone' with separate Church organizations for youth work, etc. I do not venture to dispute his conclusions, but I should like to raise a problem. Can the Church preserve a sense of identity among her members if the only specific function of the Church is worship? The old tag, 'Common Work, Common Worship, Common Witness' does crystallize an important point.

The paper contributed by Mr. Babington Smith is the centre-piece of the whole book. The previous papers have all been in the main descriptive and analytical, trying to make it clear what the facts are. Mr. Babington Smith contends that it is possible to describe the past and the present, understanding phenomena by means of the most suitable conceptual frameworks, without necessarily adopting a predestinarian view of the future: the past may seem to be 'determined' simply because we interpret it by means of laws which, it must be remembered, are descriptive, not prescriptive; for future decisions we have nevertheless a measure of freedom.

Dr. Klein contends that social drop-outs should not be regarded as just inadequate and left to rot. The discriminating reader will not be put off by the fact that she advocates a policy on sexual matters that many of us are unable to share: the really important thing about her contribution is the stress laid on the possibility of redemption and rehabilitation through acceptance. It should be made clear that 'rehabilitation' does not mean conformity to our pattern but the achievement in the fullest manner of the pattern of living most suitable to and freely chosen by the former drop-out.

Mr. Hills's paper is also concerned with the future. His distinction between 'goal language', such as 'We plan to increase the production of shoes by 3 per cent in 1970' and 'vision language' like:

'I will not cease from mental fight,
Nor shall my sword sleep in my hand
Till we have built Jerusalem
In England's green and pleasant land',

is one of several applications to discourse concerning the future of the fact that much of the language of theology is not the language of literal common sense, but the language of 'disclosure models' or of 'poetry plus', etc.

Dr. Broady's second paper faces a major problem of the 1970's: how are the universities to resolve the conflict arising from the fact that the economic system requires competent technologists, while the young men and women students are human beings and want to stay that way?

Finally, to mix our metaphors, Mr. Compton brings us down to earth with a dash of cold water: technique alone is not enough for success in industry, not even sociological (or, I would add, theological) technique. You have got to have grown into the right kind of person and to be capable of building up the right relationships with other people, in addition to having acquired the necessary technical competence.

The reader may be tempted to ask, 'What gives this book its unity?' The unity consists of the fact that each contributor shares two concerns. The first is, that human beings should live as full and mature a life together as possible in this world, whether this life is the only one we ever have, or whether it is a training for something greater. Some of us are Christians, some are not. But we have to live together and work together, so it is vital for us to understand each other. Secondly, in the near future 'social work' is going to be more and more important all over the world. Religious people often go in for work of this kind, but in this they are not alone. Many who undertake social work in one of its many forms have no religion of their own. If only for practical reasons of co-operation they ought to know something about theology and what makes religious people tick. Religious people should have a concern for all men, including 'alienated' groups, and it is important that they should have some realization of how societies tick, and this means having a rudimentary awareness of what at an academic level is called sociology. It is to help strengthen mutual understanding between religious people and those interested in sociology that this book has been written.

D. E. H. WHITELEY

I

SOCIOLOGY AND THEOLOGY:

ALIENATION AND ORIGINAL SIN

RODERICK MARTIN

There are at least three ways in which the problem of the relation between sociology and theology can be legitimately approached. From the standpoint of the sociological approach to the study of religion and religious institutions; from the standpoint of the contribution sociology can make as a technical aid to ecclesiastical effort, specifying the means whereby the Church can maximize its impact upon a specific audience; and from the standpoint of the contribution sociology can make to understanding problems theologians attempt to resolve in their own terms. This essay approaches the issue from this third standpoint; it is not concerned with the sociological interpretation of religion, nor with sociology as a manipulative aid. Instead, it attempts to indicate the type of questions social scientists address themselves to, the conceptual apparatus they use, and some of the basic theoretical questions they discuss. By doing so I hope to indicate where sociology and theology converge.

This introduction is designed to discuss these questions in more general terms than the individual papers which follow. As far as possible within the narrow confines of an introductory chapter I want to explain what sociology is, its terminology, its conceptual problems, and some of its major theories. There are innumerable sociology text-books—usually expensive and American—and I cannot hope to compress the accumulated wisdom of eighty years into 10,000 words.[1] But by concentrating upon issues relevant to a concerned Christian public, and by focussing speci-

[1] Useful American texts include: E. Chinoy, *Society: An Introduction to Sociology* (Random House, 1961); N. J. Smelser, *Sociology* (John Wiley, 1967); A. Inkeles, *What is Sociology?* (Prentice Hall, 1964). Two valuable and accessible English introductions are: P. Berger, *Invitation to Sociology: A Humanistic Perspective* (Penguin Books, 1963), a lively essay, and S. Cotgrove, *Science of Society* (Allen and Unwin, 1967), a useful introduction to British social institutions.

fically upon alienation and its origins in Christian theology, I hope to indicate possible convergences between the two disciplines, and the usefulness of dialogue between the two sides. One preliminary caution is necessary: although the paper attempts to present *the* sociological view, there remain many issues outside the sociological consensus. As will become clear, 'sociology proves' does not mean the same things as 'science proves'; rather it means 'some sociologists think'—but some thoughts are more justifiable than others.

The structure of this introduction is simple. After briefly defining sociology and discussing some of the basic issues involved in social science discussion, I attempt to sketch the outlines of the sociological tradition by focussing upon three major theorists, Durkheim, Weber, and Marx, and on later empirical work based upon their theories. The paper concludes with a discussion of the relation between the sociological concept of alienation and the theological doctrine of original sin.

i

Sociology is conventionally defined, with deceptive simplicity, as 'the study of systems of social actions and their inter-relations'.[2] The essential elements in this definition are 'social', meaning, 'involving others as well as ego', and 'system'—sometimes referred to as pattern or structure. The main significance of this definition is negative rather than positive—the exclusion of some human behaviour. It follows from the definition that the sociologist is not concerned with all human activity. If x slips on the way home from work, recovers his balance, and forgets about the incident, the event is of no interest to the sociologist (although it may be to the mathematician concerned with the techniques of probability sampling). If, on the other hand, x hurts his back, is sent to hospital, and misses work, the sociologist is interested. The first incident is excluded, the second is included, by using the term 'social' rather than 'human' behaviour, *alter* as well as *ego* is involved. Furthermore, the sociologist is concerned to discover the reason for John Smith's membership of the Congregationalist Church out of an interest in the patterns of Church attendance, not out of an interest in John Smith. The aim is to say why men who share certain characteristics belong to

[2] Cotgrove, cap. i.

certain specific denominations. Although in practice empirical sociological studies may differ only slightly from empirical historical studies, hence the narrow boundary between historical sociology and sociological history, the focus of concern is totally different. The specific sociological focus is conveyed by the use of the term 'pattern'.

The chemist is concerned with the structure of matter, the sociologist with the 'structure of social action'. What are the units of sociological analysis—the nuclei, molecules, cells and organisms of sociology? Although the precise definition of terms often varies with the theoretical framework used, there is agreement on a basic minimum of terms, the jargon of the trade. On the principle of the short, sharp shock, the following are the usual definitions of the basic terms. The basic terms in sociological jargon are 'social institution', 'social organization', and 'culture'. Social institution is defined as 'any recurrent pattern of human behaviour not explicable in biological or physical terms'; the family, marriage, the Church, the Conservative Party, and the State are all social institutions.[3] 'Social organisation' refers to 'any social unit or human group deliberately constructed and re-constructed to seek specific goals'; I.C.I., and the Transport and General Workers' Union are both social organisations. 'Culture' comprises 'the shared norms and values of members of society', while 'sub-culture' comprises the shared norms and values of a sub-group of society. Social groups, at the institutional and cultural level, are usually categorized in a number of different, related dichotomies, and history is seen as the development from the first to the second: these include traditional and rational, sacred and secular, folk and urban, communal and associational, traditional and modern. Common to all is the movement from the magical and organic to the rational and purposive.[4] And finally, the key term linking the sociological study of the group with the psychological study of the individual is 'role', usually defined as 'the behaviour expected of any individual occupying a given social position'.[5]

Definitions are necessary, but they are a necessary evil, hiding the living diversity of human behaviour in the mantle of dulled uniformity. Having briefly defined the field of sociology and the

[3] M. J. Levy, *The Structure of Society* (Princeton U.P., 1952), p. 7.
[4] Ed. T. Parsons, E. Shils, K. D. Naegele, and J. R. Pitts, *Theories of Society: Foundation of Modern Sociological Theory* (The Free Press, 1965).
[5] M. Banton, *Roles* (Tavistock Publications, 1965).

basic minimum of terms used in sociological discourse, I want to pass on to the more important and interesting task of discussing the outlines of the sociological perspective, relating the sociological study of alienation to the main stream of the sociological tradition. But before doing so, it is necessary to clarify my position regarding the status of the social sciences.

ii

The social sciences have acquired much of the prestige of the physical sciences, particularly in the United States; they are regarded as providing as accurate solutions to social problems as physical scientists provide for physical problems. Yet the social and the natural sciences are not alike. They share the hypothetico-deductive method of preliminary investigation, hypothesis, test, re-formulation, and further test. They share a common method of explanation, explaining the particular in terms of general laws and refining the laws to cover newly discovered events. They share in principle—although to such varying degrees that the differences in scale are almost differences in kind—common problems relating to the impact of the observer on the phenomena observed (and of the phenomena upon the observer), of isolating the phenomena to be observed from its environment, and of quantification.[6] However, the social scientist faces two additional problems, stemming directly from the fact that he is concerned with human behaviour, not physical events: of understanding, and of the relation between facts and values.

The explanation of human behaviour involves an act of comprehension, of understanding. The observation of objective events must be complemented by an understanding of the meaning of the behaviour for the actors themselves. Explanations of economic exchange or religious ceremonial which omit the meaning of the act for the actor are comically inadequate. 'If an observer watches a group of people who under certain circumstances exchange small pieces of paper and metal, after which one of them gives another an object which the recipient takes away, he may in due course be able to make accurate predictions about the

---

[6] The usual sources are R. B. Braithwaite, *Scientific Explanation* (Cambridge U.P., 1955); K. R. Popper, *The Poverty of Historicism* (Routledge and Kegan Paul, 1951); W. G. Runciman, *Social Science and Political Theory* (Cambridge U.P. 1963), cap. i; M. Weber, *The Methodology of the Social Sciences* (The Free Press, 1949).

transfer of goods in this community by correlating such transfers with the exchange of metal pieces. But unless the observer has grasped the ideas of money, buying and selling, and so on he cannot claim to have explained the behaviour'.[7] Similarly with religious ceremonial: explanations of Holy Communion which failed to include the symbolic significance of the breaking of the bread and the taking of wine would be meaningless. (As my three-year-old daughter commented on seeing Holy Communion on the television, 'Why are they all thirsty?')

The second problem stemming from the fact that the data of sociology are human, not physical, events is that of the relation between facts and values. Much ink has been spilt on this problem by philosophers and social scientists alike, and it is impossible to do more than state my own choice out of a number of possible alternative answers. The very terms in which social science discourse is conducted involve judgements of value; terms like 'culture', 'class', and 'status' have value connotations. Yet it is possible to separate the connotations from the core of the concept. Facts and values are, and must be, kept separate in academic discourse. 'It is said, and I agree, that politics is out of place in the lecture room . . . to take a practical political stand is one thing, and to analyze political structures and party positions is another'.[8] On the other hand, in practice moral and ideological considerations enter into sociological research, both in the choice of the subjects to be studied and often in the yard-sticks used to evaluate human behaviour. For my own part, the rigid (and ritual) commitment to the separation between facts and values seems neither necessary nor desirable: the criterion of falsifiability is applicable whatever the ideological colour of the research undertaken, and professionalism does not necessarily require intellectual emasculation.[9]

This recognition of the moral basis and implications of sociology is far from new. For the 'founding fathers' of sociology —Marx, Weber, Durkheim, Toennies and others—were inspired by essentially moral considerations: the need to comprehend, and often prevent, the corrosive effects of industrial development upon

[7] Runciman, *op, cit.*, p. 12.
[8] Ed. H. H. Gerth and C. Wright Mills, *From Max Weber* (Routledge and Kegan Paul, 1948), p. 145.
[9] A. W. Gouldner, 'Anti-Minotaur: The Myth of a Value Free Sociology', reprinted in M. Stein and M. Vidich, *Sociology on Trial* (Prentice Hall, 1963), pp. 35–52.

society and the individual. For the early sociologists were both social scientists and social critics, whether conservative (like Durkheim), moderate and pragmatic (like Charles Booth), or radical (like Marx). In their discussions of the problems of the contemporary world three themes stand out: the loss of community, the loss of a sense of mystery before the wonder of the world, and the de-humanisation of work. The first is primarily associated with the French sociologist Emile Durkheim, and centres around the concepts of social solidarity and anomie or normlessness; the second is primarily associated with the German sociologist Max Weber, and centres around the concept of rationality; and the third is primarily associated with Marx, and centres around the concept of alienation. This paper is an attempt to convey the flavour of the sociological perspective by discussing briefly these three theorists and the later use of their concepts in the analysis of twentieth century society. To illustrate the relation, both historically and substantively, between their sociology, social concern, and theology, I have paid particular attention to the concept of alienation, and to its relations with the theological doctrine of original sin.

iii

According to one recent sociological theorist, the central question sociological theory attempts to answer is: 'What is the basis of social order?'[10] How do societies cohere despite the multitude of conflicting individual and group interests they contain? Nowhere is this central focus clearer than in Durkheim's work: his central theoretical concern was with the problem of social cohesion, his central moral concern the threat rapid industrial development, individualism—'the disease of the western world'—and 'vaunted ambition' pose for individual and social integration. Industrialism, mass democracy, and secularism were destroying 'that sense of society which alone can maintain individuality'. At a group level this involved the collapse of social solidarity, at an individual level anomie or normlessness.[11]

[10] P. S. Cohen, *Modern Social Theory* (Heinemann, 1968), cap. 2.

[11] R. A. Nisbet, *The Sociological Tradition* (Heinemann, 1967), pp. 300–4. The relevant parts of Durkheim's work for the present purposes are: *The Division of Labour in Society* (Trans. by G. Simpson, The Free Press, 1933); *Suicide: A Study in Sociology* (Trans. by J. A. Spaulding and G. Simpson, Routledge and Kegan Paul, 1952); *The Elementary Forms of Religious Life* (Trans. by J. W. Swain, Routledge and Kegan Paul, 1915).

By social solidarity Durkheim meant the institutions—family, community and occupational group—and their concomitant we-feelings which held society together. History is seen as the development from mechanical solidarity, the solidarity of similarity, of moral and social homogeneity re-inforced by the discipline of the small community, to organic solidarity, the solidarity of inter-dependent difference. Modern industrial society is based upon organic solidarity, the division of labour, (although he later came to see that this pre-supposed at least a degree of homogeneity). Institutional coherence and integration is given strength and supplemented, both for the individual and for the group, by 'collective representations', especially those expressed through religious ritual. Religion, as a belief system and as a behavioural pattern, is a 'collective representation' of group life. The internalization of this collective representation and the code of behaviour it enjoins provides the basis for the specifically human elements in homo sapiens. Man is a human being in so far as he is a social being. The collapse of social solidarity, the weakening of social bonds and the emergence of discord between the individual and the group which Durkheim saw industrialisation producing caused a state of anomie or normlessness, shared by society and the individual alike.

The related concepts of social solidarity and anomie have provided the theoretical basis for much later empirical work in fields as diverse as the sociology of religion and criminology. The role of religious institutions in strengthening social solidarity and maintaining social coherence by providing symbolic representation of the group is a commonplace in social anthropology, and in diluted form informs the sociological study of religion in complex industrial societies.[12] For example, in Will Herberg, *Protestant, Catholic, Jew*, the high level of religious activity in the United States at the present time is related to the problem of integrating immigrant populations into a new nation.[13] Religious institutions help society to absorb and mould into a common framework a heterogeneous immigrant population: the Protestant, Catholic, and Jewish churches provide for individual and collective inte-

---

[12] J. Beattie, *Other Cultures* (Routledge and Kegan Paul, 1966).
[13] W. Herberg, *Protestant, Catholic, Jew* (Doubleday, 1960); G. Lenski, *The Religious Factor* (Doubleday, 1963); a useful illustration of the role of the church in providing a social home for migrant Americans is H. J. Gans, *The Levittowners* (Allen Lane: The Penguin Press, 1967), cap. iv.

gration, for underlying the surface differences between the churches is a fundamental agreement upon acceptance of the American way of life. Solidarity, and marginal differences, are reinforced simultaneously. For the individual, the high rate of geographical and social mobility which characterizes the United States has created rootlessness, a loss of community, which only some form of communal identification wider than the nuclear family, yet smaller than society as a whole, can provide.

The concept of anomie has proved even more fruitful, especially in criminological research. 'The degree of anomie in a social system is indicated by the extent to which there is a lack of consensus on norms judged to be legitimate, with its attendant uncertainty and insecurity in social relations'.[14] This lack of consensus leads to 'avoidance behaviour', and often to criminal activity. The sources of this lack of consensus lie either in society at large (normlessness understood in a strict sense, produced by society's inability to modify norms to keep pace with rapid social change), or in the conflict between different social groups, often finding expression in role conflicts within the individual (norm conflict), or in the individual himself (norm ignorance). Normlessness has been related specifically to the position of underprivileged youth in the United States and in Britain.[15] Deprived adolescents are seen as facing an inherently contradictory and consequently conflictful situation: a contradiction between the goals prescribed by society as a whole for its members, and the accessibility of legitimate means for achieving these goals. Juvenile delinquency is caused by this contradiction between the universal acceptance of the goal of material success and the lack of any legitimate means for achieving it. Inevitably, the dispossessed either repudiate the goal, as, for example, the hippies, or seek illegitimate means for achieving the goal, as in robbery with violence. Norm conflict, the second category of anomie, arises most acutely from the multiplicity of the individual's group affiliations. Individuals are members of more than one social group—or, to use slightly different language, perform more than

[14] G. Rose, 'Anomie and Deviation—A Conceptual Framework for Empirical Studies' (*British Journal of Sociology*, 1964), pp. 29 seq.

[15] R. K. Merton, *Social Theory and Social Structure* (The Free Press, 1957), caps. 4 and 5; a number of empirical studies of deviant behaviour have discussed this approach (A. B. Clinard, *Anomie and Deviant Behaviour*, The Free Press, 1964).

one role—and are likely to suffer from any conflict which may emerge from these different roles. In normal circumstances church membership and political party membership may not be incompatible: but they may be, as they were in Nazi Germany. Similarly, behaviour appropriate to the role of uncle may be in conflict with behaviour appropriate to the role of business men, for example, in the selection of applicants for a particular job. The number of examples of conflict between group memberships, and between different roles, is infinite. The result, for the individual, is internal conflict leading to 'avoidance behaviour', a stressful adjustment, or inaction. As voting studies have shown, cross pressurisation stemming from multiple group membership often results in political apathy.[16] Norm conflict may produce apathy, norm ignorance may result in simple disregard for socially prescribed behaviour. The degree to which ignorance is culpable no doubt varies but there are sections of the population ignorant of the norms governing behaviour. This is most obviously the case for example, with recent immigrants, whose knowledge of the prevailing norms is limited, and whose transgressions are accordingly frequent. Indeed, one school of thought attributes a large degree of British colour prejudice to precisely this immigrant ignorance of the unspoken norms of British life.[17] It may similarly be the case with adolescents unaware of the responsibilities of the adult role, for example over credit obligations.

The moral thread which holds Durkheim's thought together is his concern, muted but nonetheless real, with the problem of social order. Although his work has a sophisticated intellectual theoretical coherence of its own, at the risk of considerable over-simplification social solidarity and anomie can be seen within a moral and political framework. He was concerned, as is clearly revealed in his work *The Division of Labour*, with the effect of industrialism upon community, and the danger of social disintegration. With Durkheim's main English-speaking heirs, the functionalists, this concern with the problem of order is overt. Functionalists are primarily concerned to analyse social structures in terms of their function or role in sustaining the total social system: 'Society is usefully conceived as a dynamic equilibrium of various functional parts, each with its own independent function

---

[16]A. Campbell et al., *The American Voter* (John Wiley, 1960), p. 85.
[17] M. Banton, *Race Relations* (Tavistock Publications, 1967), cap. 15.

to perform for society as a whole, but each limited by, because it is inter-dependent with, the other parts'.[18] The analogy is, of course, with the human body; social institutions are, like members of the body, parts of an integrated, normally healthy whole. This very general formulation has been refined and elaborated, most notably in the work of Talcott Parsons. Parsons has attempted to specify the conditions which need to be fulfilled if society is to survive. According to Parsons all societies face the same problems, and must develop mechanisms for solving these problems if they are to survive.[19] The main problems societies must solve are: goal attainment, or agreement on 'the purpose or aim of any cycle of social action, involving decisions about the allocation of resources to particular ends'; adaptation, the acquisition of sufficient resources from the physical environment to achieve these ends; integration, the maintenance of relations between the units of the system in achieving these ends; and finally tension management, 'the problem of maintaining adequate motivation among the elements in the system and resolving tensions generated by internal interaction'. Although all social institutions help to resolve more than one of these problems, the political system is primarily concerned with goal attainment, the economy with adaptation, religious institutions with integration, and the family with tension management.

The specification of these common problems, or 'functional pre-requisites', which face society is the first step towards constructing a model of the social system. The second step involves closer discussion of relations between specific institutions and specific problems. This is, of course, an enormous task, and it has attracted the particular concern of developmental sociologists. According to the predominant view, that advanced by Clark Kerr and his colleagues, the achievement of industrial society involves solving specific problems in particular ways. Industrialization requires the acceptance of rational, scientific technology; individual achievement; geographical and social mobility; a loose-knit network; an educational system 'functionally related to the skills and professions imperative to technology . . . and not primarily

[18]A. R. Radcliffe-Brown, 'The Concept of Function', reptd. in E. F. Borgatta and H. J. Meyer, *Sociological Theory* (Knopf, 1956), pp. 263–9.
[19] T. Parsons, *The Social System* (Routledge and Kegan Paul, 1951); a useful summary of his work is R. Devereux, Jnr., 'Parsons' Sociological Theory' in ed. M. Black, *The Social Theories of Talcott Parsons* (Prentice Hall, 1964), pp. 1–63.

concerned with conserving traditional values or perpetuating the classics'; and finally a pluralist democratic political system. Whether this model of industrial society and the prescriptions for action derived from it is confirmed, or at least proven to be effective, remains to be seen. It is too early to say yet—but the American government recognized the utility of this systems approach to the extent of granting fifty million dollars to examine it more closely (only withdrawing the grant after protests by developing countries against academic imperialism).[20]

Although the fully fledged Parsonian approach has not yet been tested, attempts have already been made to apply his approach to specific institutions. The most controversial is the attempt to explain social stratification, the nature and basis of social inequality, in functionalist terms.[21] According to this functional analysis, the system of social stratification helps to solve two problems, those of adaptation and of integration. Inequality, whether material or symbolic, performs an adaptive function by providing incentives, stimulating the more able members of society to sustain the deprivations of extended training and the responsibility of performing socially important tasks. Moreover, 'to the extent that the stratification system is an expression or result of differential ranking judgements in terms of some common set of values, it serves to integrate the society. Men have a sense of justice fulfilled and of virtue rewarded when they feel that they are fairly ranked as superior and inferior by the moral standards of their own community'.

If Durkheim's major fear was that industrialization and the limitless ambition which economic life encouraged would destroy social and individual integration, Weber's main preoccupation was with the threat rationalization posed to individual autonomy. As he declared in a moving speech to the University of Munich eighteen months before his death in 1919: 'the fate of our times is characterised by rationalization and intellectualization and, above all, by the "disenchantment of the world". Precisely the ultimate and most sublime values have retreated from public life, either into the transcendental realm of mystic life or into the

[20] C. Kerr et al., *Industrialism and Industrial Man* (Heinemann, 1962), esp. p. 36; I. L. Horowitz, *The Rise and Fall of Project Camelot* (MIT, 1967).
[21] The major articles in the controversy are reprinted in R. Bendix and S. M. Lipset, *Class, Status and Power* (Routledge and Kegan Paul, 1967), pp. 47–69; B. Barber, *Social Stratification* (Harcourt, Brace and World, 1957), pp. 7–8.

brotherliness of direct and personal human relations. It is not accidental that our greatest art is intimate and not monumental, nor is it accidental that today only within the smallest intimate circles, in personal human situations, in *pianissimo*, that something is pulsating that corresponds to the prophetic pneuma, which in former times swept through the great communities like a fire-brand, welding them together. Rationality, the removal of the magical elements in human thought, was the distinctive character-istic of European development'—and the peculiar tragedy, which took almost personal form in Weber's own case.[22] It was most clearly seen in his fear that the organizational expression of rationality, bureaucracy, would destroy individual autonomy.

Bureaucracy, rationally the most efficient administrative system, is based upon two fundamental principles; predictability and impersonality. Predictability is ensured by strict adherence to the rules, impersonality by a rigid separation between official and personal life. Organizationally, bureaucracy is characterised by a functional rather than a personal relation between office-holders, a clearly defined hierarchy with a graded career structure, appointment rather than election, preferably on the basis of competitive examination, payment by fixed salaries rather than fees, and strict discipline.

In Weber's terms this is an 'ideal-type' construction. Although few bureaucracies have achieved this rational perfection, all will possess some elements and as history progresses will possess more. As a concept it has serious difficulties, including a funda-mentally ambiguous status. 'Ideal' and 'typical' are very different categories: in the present world what is ideal cannot, by definition, be typical, and what is typical cannot be ideal. Moreover, the relation between the different items in his specification is unclear.[23] Authority based upon expertise and authority based upon discipline are not necessarily the same, and may not even work in the same direction. Even more fundamentally, later empirical work suggests that predictability and efficiency, the basic criteria for bureaucracy, are not necessarily correlated. In a changing environment impersonal adherence to the rules is inefficient; in a much quoted phrase, the bureaucrat is sometimes 'fit with an unfit fitness'.

[22] Gerth and Mills, *op. cit.*, p. 155.
[23] *Ibid.*, cap. 8; R. K. Merton et al. *Reader in Bureaucracy* (The Free Press, 1952), esp. pp. 18–33.

Despite these logical difficulties Weber's discussion of legal rational authority and bureaucracy has provided the starting point for much later work, especially on organisations. Organizational theory begins with Weber, and an account of Weber's influence on the subject would be an account of the subject's history. But amongst a multitude of theoretical and empirical studies following his work A. W. Gouldner's *Patterns of Industrial Bureaucracy* remains one of the best.[24] In a case study of a gypsum mining and manufacturing plant Gouldner discovered that different environments produced different types of bureaucracy: in one situation a 'representative' bureaucracy, based upon consensus and expertise, emerged, in another a 'punishment centred' bureaucracy (resembling Weber's type), based upon authority and discipline, emerged. Moreover, he discovered that the degree of bureaucratization did not depend upon the need for efficiency, but upon political considerations, particularly the need for the new plant manager to assert his position over his predecessor's lieutenants. Rule enforcement was a result of personal uncertainty and inadequate information, not the need for efficiency. The success of rule enforcement depended upon the degree of resistance to it, which in turn was most successful in technological conditions fostering informal solidarity.

Although later research following Weber's directives has been predominantly concerned with the microscopic examination of contemporary society, he himself was primarily concerned with a broad historical sweep, attempting to discover the distinctive characteristics of Western European civilisation. The *differentia specifica* of European civilization was the distinctive role of rationality in West European culture. Its roots lay partly in specific economic conditions, the money economy and its specific European form, capitalism, and partly in a continuously evolving value system; economics and ideals worked together to enthrone rationality. Although Weber never stated his position in general terms, 'believing that historical truth would be best served by leaving general conclusions until the end of the exhaustive empirical investigation', his position was well stated in the work of one of his pupils, Otto Hinze. 'Everywhere the first impulse to social

[24]A. W. Gouldner, *Patterns of Industrial Bureaucracy* (The Free Press, 1954); a useful historical survey of recent work on bureaucracy is N. P. Mouzelis, *Organization and Bureaucracy: An Analysis of Modern Theories* (Routledge and Kegan Paul, 1967).

action is given as a rule by real interests, i.e., by political and economic interests. But ideal interests lend wings to these real interests, give them a spiritual meaning, and serve to justify them . . . in pursuing [his interest] he develops his capacities to the highest extent only if he believes that in so doing he serves a higher rather than a purely egoistic purpose. . . . Wherever interests are vigorously pursued, an ideology tends to be developed also to give meaning, reinforcement, and justification to these interests. And this ideology is as 'real' as the real interests themselves, for ideology is an indispensable part of the life process which is expressed in action. And conversely: whenever ideas are to conquer the world, they require the leverage of real interests, although frequently ideas will more or less distract these interests from their original aim . . . .'[25] That this relation between economic interest and ideal interests and their mutual inter-action is producing the distinctive tone of West European civilization, was clearly revealed in Weber's classic account of *The Protestant Ethic and the Spirit of Capitalism*. Weber defined the spirit of capitalism in terms of individual acceptance of the obligation to work regardless of extrinsic reward, which is 'calling'.[26] He was concerned to show how this secular ethic emerged from sixteenth century protestantism by relating moral attitudes to capital accumulation with theological doctrine. The religious foundations of 'worldly asceticism' and their relation to capitalist accumulation were exemplified for Weber in Richard Baxter's *Christian Dictionary*: 'If God show you a way in which you may lawfully get more than in another way, if you refuse this, and use the less gainful way, you cross one of the ends of your calling, and you refuse to be God's steward, and to accept his gifts and use them for him when he requireth; you may labour to be rich for God, but not for the flesh and sin'. Methodologically and substantively Weber's analysis is open to criticism. Methodologically, his reliance upon seventeenth and eighteenth century writers to assess the influence of sixteenth century doctrines ignores the importance of intervening developments: seventeenth century Calvinism was perverted Calvinism, not Genevan Calvinism, and reflected the adaptation of the economic ethics of the original doctrines to new circumstances.

[25] Quoted in R. Bendix, *Max Weber: An Intellectual Portrait* (Heinemann, 1960), p. 69.
[26] M. Weber, *The Protestant Ethic and the Spirit of Capitalism* (Trans. by T. Parsons, Allen and Unwin, 1930).

Substantively, his analysis ignores the Calvinist aspiration to form a 'Godly commonwealth', characterized by a stern collective discipline. In fact, Puritans tended to be 'narrow and conservative in their economic views, urging men to seek no more wealth than they needed for a modest life, or alternatively, to use up their surplus in charitable givings'. The Puritan judgement on the pursuit of money was better expressed by John Bunyan than by the (Unitarian) Benjamin Franklin; Mr. Moneylove and Mr. Sureall were thoroughly despised.[27]

Although Weber was primarily concerned with the general question of the distinctive characteristics of western civilization, his corpus includes a number of fruitful fragments. Amongst the most important is his short but perceptive analysis of the relation between class, status and power. Like Marx he defined class in economic terms: 'We may speak of a class when (1) a number of people have in common a specific causal component of their chances, in so far as (2) this component is represented exclusively by economic interests in the possession of goods and opportunities for income, and (3) is represented under the conditions of the commodity or labour markets'.[28] Unlike Marx, however, he did not regard class as the basic determinant of status, i.e. prestige, or as the basic determinant of power, i.e. the ability to obtain the compliance of others to one's own wishes independently of their own. For Weber, understanding the social structure involved understanding these three separate, but related dimensions. In many societies, for example modern capitalism, class may be the major determinant of status; but in others, for example feudalism, legal status is the determinant of class; in yet others, e.g. in contemporary Eastern Europe, political power may determine both class and status. Although this analysis of class, status and power is only a small part of Weber's work it has proved a major source of insight into the nature of modern society. According to the Marxist tradition, social class divisions retain their fundamental importance in modern capitalism, muted but not obliterated by the increase in wealth for the proletariat. The working classes remain powerless and deprived. However, society can no longer be

---

[27] M. Waltzer, *The Revolution of the Saints* (Weidenfeld and Nicholson, 1966), pp. 304–5.
[28] Gerth and Mills, *op. cit.*, p. 181; W. L. Warner and P. S. Lunt, *The Social Life of a Modern Community* (Yale U.P., 1941): W. L. Warner, *Structure of American Life* (Edinburgh U.P., 1952), caps. 1 and 2.

analysed in these simple dichotomous economic terms. For class conflict has been replaced by individual status seeking, status being indicated by a particular way of life and its evaluation by others. This view is evident most clearly in the United States, where more attention has been paid both by sociologists and the population at large to status strata than to economic classes. In W. L. Warner's study of *Yankee City* the community was divided into six social strata, each consisting of individuals symbolically placed by the majority of the population. Social position depended upon the group which admitted you, and the evaluation of your position by the community; the criteria for evaluation were multiple, including length of residence in the community, type of house, and general way of life. Income was not a direct determinant of status.

If the fear of social disintegration preoccupied Durkheim and the aweful clarity of the disenchanted world Weber, the moral thread running through Marx's work is the dehumanisation and alienation of the worker under capitalism. Marx's rejection of Hegel, his critique of capitalism, and his vision of a Communist Utopia is informed by the sight of alienated man and the vision of unalienated man. For Marx, alienation involved man's experience of himself as the passive object of external forces, not as a self-activating agent. 'Man does not experience himself as the acting agent in his grasp of the world, but that the world (nature, others and himself) remain alien to him.'[29] Although alienation was to be found in all areas of social life, including politics and religion, it was to be found most acutely in the world of work. Man is alienated from himself as a 'species being', from other men, from the act of production, and from the product of his labour. As Marx movingly wrote in the *Economic and Philosophical Manuscripts in 1844*, 'in what does this alienation of labour consist? First, that the work is *external* to the worker, that it is not a part of his nature, that consequently he does not fulfil himself in his work but denies himself, has a feeling of misery, not of well-being, does not develop freely a physical and mental energy, but is physically exhausted and mentally debased. The worker, therefore, feels himself at home only during his leisure, whereas at work he feels

---

[29] T. Bottomore and M. Rubel, *Karl Marx: Selected Writings in Sociology and Social Philosophy* (Penguin Books, 1963), pp. 175–86; R. Nisbet, *op. cit.*, pp. 284–92.

homeless. His work is not voluntary but imposed, *forced labour*. It is not the satisfaction of a need, but only a means for satisfying other needs. Its alien character is clearly shown by the fact that as soon as there is no physical or other compulsion it is avoided like the plague. Finally, the alienated character of work for the worker appears in the fact that it is not his work but work for someone else, that in work he does not belong to himself but to another person'.

Alienated labour derives ultimately from commodity fetishism, the money economy, and private property. Labour becomes externalized as a commodity: 'The product of labour is labour which has been embodied in an object, and turned into a physical thing; this product is an *objectification* of labour. The performance of work is at the same time its objectification. This performance of work appears, in the sphere of political economy, as a vitiation of the worker, objectification as a loss. . .' 'The worker puts his life into the object, and his life then belongs no longer to him but to the object . . . what is embodied in the product of his labour is no longer his . . . the alienation of the worker in his product means not only that his labour becomes an object, takes on its own existence, but that it exists outside him, independently . . . and that it stands opposed to him as an autonomous power'. Money, as the medium of exchange, 'the reflection in a single commodity of the value relations between all commodities', symbolizes this subordination to external objects. As Marx declared, 'money is the jealous One God of Israel, beside which no other God may stand. Money dethrones all the gods of man and turns them into a commodity. Money is the universal, independently constituted value of all things. It has, therefore, deprived the whole world, both the world of man and nature, of its value. Money is the alienated essence of man's work and his being. This alien being rules over him and he worships it.'[30] It is the expropriation of this externalised object by the bourgeoisie which constitutes the peculiar exploitation of capitalism; it was this expropriation, and thus exploitation, which would cease with the socialist revolution, and the emancipation of society from private property.

In recent years alienation has become a popular catchword, a portmanteau concept covering everything from individual Angst

[30] Quoted in R. Tucker, *Philosophy and Myth in Karl Marx* (Cambridge U.P., 1965), p. 111.

to general social disintegration. As one sociologist commented, 'it has become a popular vehicle of virtually every kind of analysis, from the prediction of voting behaviour to the search for *The Sane Society*.' It has been used to refer to an objective social condition, one in which the system of social relations is characterized by money fetishism, to an individual's experience of his relations with the external world, and to an individual state of mind.[31] At a social psychological level it refers to the 'sense of the splitting asunder what was once together, the breaking of the seamless mould in which values, behaviour, and expectations were once cast into interlocking forms', and at a psychological level to the neurotic disintegration of the personality. Indeed one writer has gone so far as to argue, 'Alienation is used to convey the emotional tone which accompanies any behaviour in which the person is compelled to act self-destructively'.[32] Despite the difficulties which this widespread use of the concept creates, it still remains possible to use the term in a strictly sociological context, and to relate it to empirical research. By ignoring the ontological ante-cedents of the concept, by discarding Marx's programmatic prescriptions but retaining his socio-historical emphasis, by replacing property relations with the division of labour, and by breaking the concept down into its constituent elements and elaborating them, it is possible to use the concept of alienation as a sociological tool, as sociologists like Melvin Seeman and especi-ally Robert Blauner, have done.

Alienation refers to a syndrome of 'objective conditions and subjective feeling states'.[33] It comprises a state of mind associated with a given external social situation, and that social situation itself. The state of mind comprises four distinct categories of fragmentation: powerlessness, meaninglessness, isolation, and self-estrangement. A person experiences powerlessness when he is an object controlled and manipulated by other persons or by an impersonal system such as technology, and when he cannot assert himself as a subject to change or modify this domination. A person

[31] M. Seeman, 'On the Meaning of Alienation', reprinted in L. Coser and B. Rosenberg, *Sociological Theory: A Book of Readings* (Macmillan (N.Y.), 1957), p. 526; S. M. Lukes, 'Alienation and Anomie', in W. G. Runciman and P. Laslett, *Politics, Philosophy and Society*, 3rd series (Basil Blackwell, 1967), p. 136.
[32] L. Feuer, 'What is Alienation? The Career of a Concept', reptd. in Stein and Vidich, *op. cit.*, p. 143.
[33] R. Blauner, *Alienation and Freedom* (Chicago U.P., 1964), passim.

experiences meaninglessness when his actions seem to have no relation to a broader life programme, or when his activities do not seem to have any organic connection with the whole of which they are a part. Isolation comprises 'the feeling of being in, but not of, society, a sense of remoteness from the larger social order, an absence of loyalties to intermediate collectivities'. Finally, self-estrangement refers to the experience of work as being a means to an end rather than an end in itself, and a heightened awareness of time resulting from a split between present engagements and future considerations. All these four items are to be discovered in the modern industrial work situation. In modern industry the worker experiences powerlessness, for his speed of work is dictated by the machine he is operating, and the individual expertise of the craftsman has been built into the machine. Meaninglessness stems from the individual's fragmented relation to his work; the subdivision of tasks has diminished the area of understanding as well as responsibility. The worker is isolated both from the product of his labour by the non-ownership of the product produced, and often from his fellow workers by the layout of the factory. Finally, the worker is self-estranged; work has become an instrumental activity subordinated to the most animal needs for food and shelter, rather than an end in itself. Alienation, in these terms, can be viewed as the result of employment in large-scale enterprises, and the division of labour, rather than as a result of capitalist exploitation. It is the task of the industrial sociologists to relate these feelings and experiences to specific industrial situations.

The objective conditions which cause alienation are basically determined by industrial technology and market forces. Different types of industrial technology allow industrial workers varying degrees of power, meaning, and integration within the work place. In a craft technology, like the printing industry and parts of the building industry, alienating conditions are at a minimum: the lack of standardisation of the product prevents the rationalization of the work process, preserving the individual worker's discretion. The printer largely sets his own pace of work, can readily see the meaning of his own activity in relation to the whole process, and is integrated into a meaningful occupational community. The standardization of the product in mass consumption industries like the textile and car industries produces a very different situation. Expertise is built into the machine, limiting the discretion of the individual worker, individual tasks are minutely sub-divided parts of a whole, and the worker is isolated from his fellow workers. In both 'machine minding' technologies like the textile industry and assembly line technologies like the car industry the worker's experience of powerlessness, meaninglessness, and isolation is most acute. The worker's powerlessness 'is expressed in a constant work pressure and inability to control movement, meaninglessness in a fragmented production process, and isolation in lack of contact with others and lack of commitment to institutional goals'. However, this experience is not universal in modern industry. In contrast to the textile and motor car industries the chemical and petroleum industries, characterized by a continuous process technology, offer their work force considerable freedom from pressure, control over their pace of work, responsibility for maintaining a high quality product, choice of how to do the job, and the freedom of physical movement. Although the individual worker no longer uses his individual skill to manufacture a product, he retains discretion over the allocation of his own time and effort. In continuous process technology the worker's main task is to ensure that the process is operating smoothly by watching instruments, and where breakdowns occur seeing that maintenance staff are called. Responsibility replaces skill as a source of the worker's human dignity, and of his self-realization.

Blauner's approach to the study of alienation and its roots in modern industrial technology is derived directly from Marx. Like Marx, he holds up an image of what the work role might be, and sees that in many situations reality falls short of his image. The industrial worker should be an autonomous, integrated individual, discovering meaning and self-realization in the work place. Instead, he is often the passive object of industrial technology, a mutilated fragment in a domineering process he does not understand. In approaching the subject in this way Blauner raises a crucial question for social scientists, the role of values in social science. For some critics, the important question is not the actual as compared with the ideal, but the actual as compared with the participant's expectations. Whether a given technology is alienating or not depends upon the actor, as well as upon the actual situation. Alienation occurs when work expectations are not fulfilled, not when the situation fails to measure up to some ideal. Where workers have adjusted their expectations to the reality of the work situation, expecting little, it is a waste of time to discuss alienation in Marxist terms. As a recent investigation into a British car plant revealed, many car workers have a purely 'instrumental orientation' to their work, regarding it as a means towards an end not as an end in itself.[34] They expect work to be financially rewarding, not to be interesting, and will be more disappointed by inadequate financial rewards than with dreary work—they expect work to be dreary.

Yet this 'accepting' attitude towards the social structure is a sharp departure from the 'classical' attitude towards social research. As we have seen, the works of Durkheim, Weber, and Marx reveal clearly the inseparability of social diagnosis and social research. The concepts which have provided the basis for the most fruitful modern research, including the most self-consciously objective empirical research, were initially presented as part of a critique of contemporary society that was often moral and ideological in origin. The continued importance in the sociological perspective of concepts like social solidarity, anomie, rationality, legal rational authority, bureaucracy and alienation illustrates one simple truth: above the most elementary level it is only possible to understand what is by envisaging what might be—and to understand what might be by discovering what is. Nowhere is this clearer than with the concept of alienation.

iv

On its first emergence in the early nineteenth century sociology 'inherited the unresolved dilemmas of traditional metaphysics'.[35] It has attempted, in its own way, to solve them ever since. Nowhere is this doubt and this struggle clearer than in the discussion of the industrial work role and the analysis of alienation. A direct line can be drawn from Christian theology via Hegel and Marx to modern sociology. As Philip Rieff has remarked, 'alienation was originally neither a Marxist nor a psychiatric tool of understanding the human condition, but theological and specifically

[34] J. H. Goldthorpe et al., *The Affluent Worker: Industrial Attitudes and Behaviour* (Cambridge U.P., 1968).

[35] G. Lichtheim, 'Alienation' in *International Encyclopaedia of the Social Sciences* (Collier-Macmillan, 1967), vol. 1, p. 268.

Christian'.[36] The concept of alienation has its origin in the parable of the Fall of Man. 'In the act of cognition—of desiring to become something more or other than what one might merely continue to be—the old Adam disobeyed God and thereby became estranged from the Divine in himself'. In the original Christian doctrine this alienation of man from God, and from himself ('self-estrangement'), can only be overcome by accepting divine forgiveness through Christ, and obedience to the divine commandment 'love thy neighbour as thyself'. There is a clear path from the Old Testament to Marx, through St. Paul, Augustine, Luther and Hegel.

The pre-Marxist history of the concept of alienation is more interesting to historians of philosophy than to sociologists, but a short discussion of the relation between Hegel and Marx will be enough to reveal the metaphysical and philosophical roots of the sociological concept. For Hegel alienation was 'an ontological fact, in the structure of grammar as well as of life, for the self, the individual, was not just an 'I' seeking to shape the world according to its intentions, but also a 'me', an object whose identity is built up by the picture that *others* have of 'me''.[37] Man is both subject, striving to control his own fate, and object, manipulated by others. Human consciousness had externalized itself in spirit; it was man's task to repossess the externalized object and to be born again, reintegrated. For Marx, Hegel's concern only with the spirit, and explanation of alienation in human nature, was inadequate. Marx explicitly translated alienation from the realm of Hegelian philosophy to that of socio-economic development, and sociology.

In Marx's hands the concept of alienation became a tool of social analysis and social criticism. Under capitalism man's condition was one of alienation, and exploitation, of submission to the tyranny of external objects, appropriated by others. Man's future condition could be one of self-realization, of freedom and spontaneity. Proletarian revolution, which would bring the machinery of bourgeois exploitation crashing down, would usher in a new social order and a new man. Subsequent writers have discarded the political programmes which would bring this ideal state nearer, but have retained the vision, and the contrast between

[36] P. Rieff, *The Triumph of the Therapeutic* (Chatto and Windus, 1966), pp. 206–7.
[37] D. Bell, *The End of Ideology* (Collier Books, 1961), p. 358.

the vision and reality. Without it sociology and social criticism would be considerably poorer.

It was a common concern with the apparent alienation of men in the contemporary world which united the very diverse participants in the conference. Although we did not spend our time bewailing the wickedness of the world, we shared a common interest in analysing the causes of our present discontents and looking for a way forward. To some social scientists this may seem a betrayal of scientific objectivity, a retreat from scientific sociology into the old-fashioned humanist tradition. But in fact it is simply a restatement of the 'classical' view, a view which has proved more fruitful than more modern, and more anaemic, attitudes. There is no contradiction between the social science method and traditional philosophical and humanitarian concerns: the criteria of falsifiability are as applicable to hypotheses concerning the industrial worker's alienation as they are to less value-laden problems. And criticism based upon objective facts is obviously preferable to criticism based upon random anecdotes.

As we have seen, sociology has developed historically from the philosophical, moral, and political concerns of the early nineteenth century, of the years following the French and industrial revolutions. It drew its theoretical concepts from sources as diverse as Christian theology, enlightenment rationalism, German idealism, the conservative reaction to the French and industrial revolutions, and many others. In recent years there has been a tendency to deny this past condition, to maintain a self-consciously value-free stance, asserting sociology's scientific status, disciplinary autonomy, and distinctiveness from political ideologies like socialism with which it had been wrongly associated. This period of insecure aggressiveness is, hopefully, now over. Substantial scientific achievements, and substantial institutional safeguards, fortify its present status. Perhaps sociology, social diagnosis, social, political and moral philosophy, and moral theology can once more come together, as they did in the writings of the classic nineteenth century theorists.

In the guise of an introductory essay to a volume of essays intended for the general, socially concerned, predominantly religious public, I have attempted to show how far sociology has been concerned with important social issues. By illustrating the fusion between social research and social criticism in the classic nineteenth century writers and their more empirical descendants, rather than by an empirical account of current social problems, I have attempted to show how 'relevant' sociology is for the socially conscious Christian. By illustrating the metaphysical roots of the sociological concept of alienation—the concept which serves to unite the different contributions to this conference—I have suggested that sociologists have, whether they recognise it or not, a common heritage with theology, and that they might profitably look to their past, present and future in company with theologians. Sociology and theology both share a common concern in understanding and explaining human behaviour, and especially contemporary social problems. They both provide 'models' for the explanation of such behaviour (although I do not claim to understand the status of theological models). As became clear in the discussion of alienation and original sin during the conference proceedings, the human experience which sociologists explain in terms of social forces the theologian explains in terms of parable. Both modes of explanation are valid in their own terms, and in terms of a common usefulness in providing guide-lines for the future.

II

CHRISTIAN SOCIAL RESPONSIBILITY

THEOLOGICAL AND SOCIOLOGICAL CRITERIA[1]

MAURICE BROADY

Action, to be soundly based, needs to be guided not by hunch but by clearly worked out rational criteria. Of these criteria, in this connection, there are two kinds. Theological criteria derive from a concept of the *esse* of the Church and specify what the Church *ought* to be doing; while sociological criteria spell out much more empirically what the situation of the Church, regarded sociologically as a voluntary society, actually *is* in modern society. Policy derives from the tension between an understanding of what is and a striving after what ought to be the case. Both kinds of criteria are needed and each complements the other. In defining ecclesiastical activity, theological considerations are obviously more mandatory than are sociological, but they tend to be very general. Sociological criteria, on the other hand, are more specific but, conversely, less obligatory upon the Church. A soundly based policy for social responsibility would be one which took full account of both kinds of criteria.

(1) *Theological Criteria*

Christ came into the world both to reconcile man to God and to enable man to achieve his destiny in God's design—i.e. to have the double relationship of loving obedience to God and loving fellowship with man. This is what it means to be truly human; and this true humanity was in fact exhibited, and may be said to have been achieved, in Christ's earthly life, in the face of evil.

He is thus 'the proper Man', and his relationship to the society about him was threefold:

1. In himself he exemplified *true humanity*, regardless of whether or not it was acknowledged as such.

[1] Reprinted from *Crucible*, the journal of the Church Assembly Board, for Social Responsibility, May 1967.

2. He exercised the powers of true humanity towards *his* fellow men in activities such as prophecy, teaching, healing, forgiving. These activities

(*a*) sprang out of his unique insight or discernment (*theoria*) about human life—a discernment deriving from his relationship with the Father,

(*b*) exhibited the two qualities of authoritative power (*exousia*) —in that he obeyed God and so exercised God's *exousia*—and of service (*diakonia*)—in that he acted always for the good of men.

3. By calling men into fellowship and allegiance with himself (*koinonia*).

Underlying this ministry was the note of Judgment of the evil, and Fulfilment of the good in society. The Church, therefore, has the same three functions:

1. It acts as a model for society.

2. It acts towards men with *exousia* and *diakonia*, its action springing from the distinctive *theoria* which is given by its relationship with Christ. (It is this *theoria* which gives the characteristic Christian 'bloom' to Church activities and which makes it possible to ask if there is an unique and distinctive characteristic to social activities performed by the Church.)

3. It calls others into fellowship, and thus into their own humanity, in Christ.

The ultimate aim is that all should be drawn into this fellowship so that Church and society become one, whether this is expressed as the Church assimilating society or society assimilating the Church. In the present, Church and society are distinct bodies, although the members of the former all belong to the latter: and this distinction is the context within which Christians are called to exercise these fundamental social responsibilities. Whether or not a Church at any one time or in any one society should be acting with or over against society is not a subject on which any general theological answer can be given. This is a matter for 'situationally relevant' judgments which take full account of the particular, historically determined circumstances of the age. Much depends upon how far the objectives and the institutional arrangements of society accord, at any given time and place, with a Christian doctrine of man.

The Church, as the agency through which these obligations are to find expression, is an institution in the sense that it has a corporate name, an identity and a tradition expressed in a history of corporate thought and common conciliar decisions. It stands under an obligation to express the Christian truths about men both by service and by teaching and prophecy. The Church is represented primarily within the *local* community. Evangelism is the purpose of the Church, and it has often been supposed that its prime function in relation to society was constantly, and in a rather narrow sense, to 'name Christ'. In our view, however, it is more important to express the Church's compassionate concern for man rather than simply to use every occasion to proselytize.

Secondly, while the Church is properly thought of in organic terms as a 'body corporate', in practice people are apt to regard it either as an institution or pattern of organization or hierarchy on the one side, or as a collection of individual members on the other. Clearly, these are not mutually inconsistent viewpoints; but differences of outlook will follow according to which element in the structure of the Church is stressed and held prior to the other. What might be called the institutional view is coming under increasing criticism while the active role of the laity is being stressed. One of the major points around which the subsequent argument proceeds is the awareness of the importance of lay involvement in the Church's activities.

The Church and social work

A number of arguments have been advanced in support of the view that if the Church is to express its concern for social welfare, it must have some organization of its own through which to do so. At one time one of the reasons advanced for undertaking moral welfare work was the possibility of evangelism which it was thought likely to make possible. But this kind of expectation is hardly viable.

A second line of argument has been referred to in Barbara Rodgers' review in *Crucible* of *The Church in Social Work* by M. P. Hall and I. V. Howse (Routledge and Kegan Paul, 1965). Mrs. Rodgers states that 'There is a good deal in the argument that unless the Church has its own organization for social work and is involved in some measure in social *action*, in providing some on-going social service, its social concerns may dry up or reach no further than the somewhat negative approach of denouncing social evils'. This argument, however, can hardly be sustained.

For the facts are that very many Christians actively engage in social work in the statutory agencies as an expression of their Christian concern, and that they, like most Church people, are singularly unaware of the social work done by the Church.

A third argument might be that the Church is a caring, as well as a witnessing, community, and that it must therefore show itself not only in words but in deeds. This would imply that the Church itself should undertake social work under its own *aegis*. This kind of argument has been associated with what has earlier been called an institutional view of the Church. If, however, the Church is regarded as its members, both clerical and lay, then it can be argued that the laity are acting *as* the Church, in working out their Christian concerns in secular social work agencies. From this point of view, therefore, a social work organization run specifically by the Church itself would not be necessary, since the Church would be carrying out social work through its own members inspired with Christian sympathies and insights.

At the moment, however, the Church is finding it very difficult to bear the cost of the existing work and to find suitably qualified workers to undertake it at the salaries which can be afforded. The implications of this kind of observation are more compelling if it is accepted that there is no reason why the statutory services should not do moral welfare work as well as if not better than the Church itself. The statutory authorities are generally able to offer salaries and conditions of service which make it easier for them than for the Church to employ professional workers in social welfare, who are both well trained and expert in their fields. The local Church, on the other hand, is now unable to employ sufficient workers at a good enough rate of remuneration to provide an adequate and efficient service. It might, therefore, be felt to be an inappropriate use of the Church's scarce resources for it to attempt to do what, even in the field of distinctively personal social service, could equally well be undertaken by the social welfare workers employed by the local authorities.

From the point of view of the Church itself, it can also be argued that it should give up its existing social work organization since it might stand in danger of losing its freedom of action by becoming excessively trammelled with what has been called 'a fossilizing organization'. It might well be more appropriate to regard the role of the Church in social service as pioneering and

D

sparking off ideas which other organizations would then administer, in the same way that the Friends' Relief Service was instrumental in setting up Oxfam, which is now quite independent of the Society of Friends.

These arguments lead to the conclusion that the existing pattern of social work, restricted as it is to the Church's traditional concern for moral welfare, should now be given up on the grounds that such work could equally well be done by the statutory authorities; that, on its present resources, the Church cannot be expected to maintain a social service that can count as efficient by comparison; and that there are many other compelling demands which the Church could try to meet in its desire to express its concern for social responsibility.

It is, however, important to note that these arguments do not apply to the Church's activity *in toto* but to one particular kind of activity in terms of which the Church has hitherto tended to acquit itself of its concern for social welfare. Though these arguments have been largely pragmatic, it must be remembered that there are issues of principle involved which would entirely justify the Church in seeking to find new ways of expressing this responsibility. In the first place, theologically, there are matters of Grace which lie outside the sphere of civil legislation and thus are not properly within the purview of the State: secondly, this theological formulation entails a pluralist approach to social organization which regards Society as different and distinctive from the State and which implies that responsibility and initiative within a democracy should be shared between these two sectors of corporate life. A democracy is that kind of society in which a plurality of groupings and associations quite outside the State exercise clear areas of authority. These two principles also justify the Church in seeking to find a means of expressing its concern for social well-being in ways other than those which are at present carried out by the State itself. The Church's activity in this regard is more important at the present time since there is an inevitable increase in the centralization of power and governmental control in so many spheres of public life. This tendency is, however, being offset by the growth in the number of educated citizens who are ready and able to criticize and appraise the State's actions. It is in this wider political context that the role of the laity within the Church assumes a particular importance at the present time.

(2) *Sociological Criteria*

It is, therefore, necessary to re-think the terms in which the Church's social concern shall best be expressed in contemporary terms. This is the point at which consideration needs to be given to the sociological criteria which bear upon this problem. The characteristics of the Church in its relation to the wider society which appear to be relevant to this line of thinking are:

(i) The Christian tradition has placed great emphasis upon service; the Church is both a caring and a witnessing community. Indeed, it has been suggested that the Church's distinctive role is to express 'therapeutic love' in the community.

(ii) Nowadays many Christians express their social concern less through work within the Church itself than through their work as professional social workers in the statutory social services, right outside the framework of the institutional Church. While it is important to acknowledge the desirability of professionalism as an element in the efficient conduct of social work, this should not lead to an uncritical acceptance of professionalism as *ipso facto* virtuous; nor should it lead to the undervaluing of the contribution which voluntary, non-professional people may be able to make in spheres like this.

(iii) Many other Christians, who may or may not be professionally qualified, also wish to express this same concern for social welfare and do so in all manner of neighbourly good works, as part of what Canon Lloyd has called 'the Church's ambulance work'.

(iv) The Anglican Church covers the country with a parochial system; it is ubiquitous; it has its 'contact-men' everywhere.

(v) The Church has tended to be, and in many cases still is, closely associated with the political and economic power system of our society. It is nevertheless possible for it, if it so chooses, to claim a degree of impartiality and independence within that power structure and thus to have a distinctive stance from which to comment upon the operation of the society within which it finds itself.

(3) *A Policy for Social Responsibility*

A policy for social responsibility should take full account of these criteria in trying to interpret how the Church should fulfil its obligation both to be of service to men and to exercise authority within its society. The five points of a possible policy which follow, therefore, correspond exactly with the five points which have been spelled out above. The general aim of a policy for social responsibility should be to develop the Church's work as a sounding board of Christian opinion and a springboard of Christian social action. It might try to work along the following lines:

(i) Given that the Church stands in a continuous tradition of social service and concern, the object of the Council of Social Responsibility should be to foster thought and action about the implications of that tradition.

(ii) Given that many Christians operate as professional social workers, the object should be to strengthen in their expression of this tradition of social concern the very many Church people who are working and seeking to express their sense of Christian responsibility outside the institutional Church, typically in the statutory social services. The purpose of this enterprise should be to help Christians to consider their daily work and the problems which it brings in the light of a Christian view of man and society.

(iii) Since many people wish to express this concern in neighbourly good works, the Council should try to assist the layman to make this contribution within the parishes a good deal more effectively than is at present being done.

(iv) Since the Church is ubiquitous, the Council should seek to develop common policies which would make it possible to co-ordinate the activities of the separate parishes which at present often operate the less effectively for being singularly individualistic in outlook and organization.

(v) If the Church can claim impartiality for its judgments, this very distinctive characteristic should be used more constructively in the local society. In trying to do this the Council would clearly need to bring together with the clergy the experience of laymen in all walks of life, in order to assess local situations in the light of both theological and technical criteria.

Diakonia and exousia

The first major point which underlies this policy concerns the relationship and balance between *diakonia* and *exousia*. The definition of service formulated by the World Council of Churches made clear the close relationship between witness and service. 'The power of service is given by the Holy Spirit who uses the Church as his instrument in manifesting the Kingdom of God and Lordship of Jesus Christ in all human relations and all social structures. Service thus is a part of adoration of God and witnesses to His love for us and all men.' *Exousia* and *diakonia*, therefore, are inseparable. However, they are apt to become separated in practice, no doubt because the practice of good works is a much more intelligible and direct expression of the Church's concern for its fellow men than the practice of critical judgment. Certainly, in the Church of England, *diakonia* has tended to be emphasized while, at the local level in particular, the Church's criticial or judicial function has been largely left to go by default. In a society whose basic philosophy is pragmatic and utilitarian, this is perhaps understandable. While a good deal of practical social work still remains to be done by Church people, it is also important to emphasize the Church's judicial function: and this means that the Church must grew in the discernment (*theoria*) out of which both *exousia* and *diakonia* must spring.

Impartiality

Secondly, the effective exercise of *exousia* depends upon the acceptance of the Church's claim to be impartial. The Church shares the ordinary economic life of the society in which it is part and it may well be that today it is becoming more dependent than ever upon the economic power system, particularly where it has penetrated society in some depth as it has done in the fields of education and social work. The whole financial organization of the Church of England is deeply rooted in the economic structure of society. In most areas of social policy arguments take place between groups which manifestly have vested interests at stake. In many such areas, however, if the Church could establish its claim to be genuinely independent, then the viewpoint which it might be able to contribute to such arguments might well be respected and valued. Its position, in this respect, is very similar to that of a university which, while obviously dependent on the State and the economy for its existence and well-being, can often substantiate a claim for the impartiality of its judgments.

For this, however, the Church needs to have sufficient expertise at its disposal to talk about the problems on which it is commenting. As Gordon Dunstan put it, 'Talk from the sidelines in professional matters is often worse than useless'. It has to have contact with a sufficient number of knowledgeable people engaged in secular activities to give it access to the knowledge and experience which is needed. The Church should therefore try to bring together active Christians and sympathizers who could relate their expertise to their Christian concerns.

The judgments which the Church might wish to make would almost inevitably entail making critical assessments of the work of public bodies. At national level, this is already being done through the preparation of reports and the close contact which it is possible to sustain, for example, with the two Houses of Parliament. At local level, however, this would be more difficult, for local authorities appear to be much less willing than the national government to consult voluntary bodies, still less to take their opinions into account in making decisions. The local authorities, furthermore, are particularly likely to call in question the Church's credentials for judging what they are doing. This is not a position which can readily be endorsed, since it appears to imply that the local authority cannot legitimately be criticized by interested groups outside itself. In such matters, the Church stands in the same position as any other well-informed pressure group. However, the more representative the Church is, the more likely it is to be attended to with interest and respect. The local Anglican Church alone would carry much less weight, and would be listened to with much less respect, if it made pronouncements on publicly controversial issues, however well sustained by expertise, than would similar pronouncements coming from a local Council of Churches.

Christian understanding

The third point concerns the role which the Church might have in helping Christians and sympathizers to understand their daily work in the light of a view of life broader than purely professional theory. While the job of the social worker or the administrator, for example, is professionally defined, they have areas of discretionary action in which their personal judgment comes into play. This area of discretion makes possible the development of an *individual style* in the conduct of affairs which is influenced by *personal* outlook as much as by professional requirements. If the Church has something distinctive to contribute by way of concern for dispassionate service, for example, or for reconciliation, this needs to be considered in relation to professional activity.

The professional or the social worker, furthermore, may often be under considerable stress, emotionally, intellectually and spiritually. Very often it is impossible to express this stress in the professional context itself, in the office or the case conference. Nor do the exigencies of administration encourage people to reveal the strains under which they are operating. These can probably only be freely expressed in an entirely impartial, non-official but sympathetic atmosphere. The Church might try to create such an atmosphere in which people could come together regularly in order to clear their minds about the difficulties they confront in their professional tasks. The object of such activity would be to foster a continuous process of re-thinking not only of social work and other professional practice but also of the problems confronting the manual worker on the shopfloor, through the use of group discussion both to consider problems and to help formulate new conceptions of professional practice. Such an enterprise would be the more valuable for being inter-professional.

The worshipping Church

All these new activities which have been proposed presuppose the continuing role of the Church as a worshipping community with its own distinctive, corporate existence over and above that of its individual members. As such, the institutional Church and its tradition constitutes the source of the distinctive vision which underlies both aspects of the Church's engagement with the secular world; and which permits the Church to speak particularly to the condition of those whose circumstance cannot be altered or alleviated by social welfare work. In such circumstances, where authoritativeness is useless and practical service ineffective, the Church's vision of the nature of man enables Christians to deepen men's insight into their situation.

III

POWER, AUTHORITY AND CONFLICT

MALCOLM C. GOLDSMITH

Powerless Man?

Today's society has often been accused of dehumanizing man and making him powerless, of taking away his individuality, of making him a number, or a cog in a machine. Those who would take up this viewpoint can find many illustrations to back their accusations. They can point to the way in which government departments often refer to us by numbers and codes; as, for instance, for the purposes of National Insurance I am known as ZY/97/83/47/B. But this is not only to be found in government; for the purposes of my rented television set I am No. 124559. People can also point to the decline in small family businesses and the growth of great combines. Particularly is this relevant in the sphere of the family grocer, where Mr. Brown and his local knowledge and gossip has given way to Fine Fare and Tesco. Perhaps Autobuffets and the like are but a natural progression from this. Yet again, people can point to the fact that more and more, in our modern society, emphasis is placed upon paper qualifications, and only then upon personal initiative and personality. So much so, that even in secondary education, it has been found necessary in recent years to bring in the C.S.E. examinations, as a sort of second-class G.C.E. Certainly the idea of dehumanization is to be found within the university world, with the government declaring that in the year nineteen seventy something we shall need so many thousand technologists, so many thousand graduates in this, that or the other discipline. We are rapidly reaching the stage where the university careers of people will be settled to a certain extent, whilst the pupils are still in the Infants School. And so I could go on; the examples that can be found are legion.

This process of cutting a man down to size, though, has not altogether been to the detriment of the ordinary working man. Whilst it is true that the average citizen is surrounded by powers of government, national and local, and is made fodder for the gigantic animals of the commercial world, it is also true that he has been freed from the often ruthless exploitation imposed upon him by industrialists and governments of the nineteenth century. There can be few working men who, despite their contemporary frustrations and problems, would wish to turn the clock back very many years. This society, which has been accused of dehumanizing man, has also been responsible for freeing him from irresponsible power, and at last placing his feet on the ladder which may eventually lift him to freedom, responsibility and maturity.

It should not be thought that the ordinary man is powerless in the face of this rapidly changing society. This is not to say that he has sufficient power, nor to say that he yet realizes just what powers are at his disposal, and what could be accomplished if he were to harness them. I want to pinpoint just four examples of different kinds of power that can be exercised by the 'dehumanized masses'. This list is not intended to be exhaustive, and you may well be able to think of other, and better examples.

Firstly, the power of the unofficial, wildcat strike. Such actions have so often been vilified, sometimes quite correctly, but this power to disrupt, which may occasionally be a mis-use of power, can be of tremendous value to the morale of men. The possibilities of the unofficial strike are a constant reminder to men that *they* are important, and that whatever the authorities, whether of Management or of the Unions, say, ultimately they can assert their own individuality. It is very doubtful whether the move by certain influential people to make official strikes illegal is a progressive step at all.

Secondly, the power of the neighbourhood. Perhaps one of the greatest social problems in Britain today is that of the declining neighbourhood with all the ancillary problems that this presents. In some areas of the country action by local residents and interested parties has brought interesting results; for instance, take this incident, recounted by Christopher Holmes for the Student Christian Movement.[1] 'Colville Gardens, London, W.11, is the focal point of the Notting Hill People's Association. Over the past months, each Saturday, cars from the Portobello market have invaded the street, not only by parking down the road-kerbs, but

[1] In a preparatory pamphlet written for the S.C.M. Conference on 'Power' in December, 1967.

by triple parking—down the centre. It was dangerous for the children: no car could see a child dashing out (and the pavement is the only place to play); it was dangerous in case of emergency—no ambulance or fire-engine could have gained access; and it was illegal. But the police said it was only a low priority. So the People's Association decided to take action themselves. At 9 a.m. on Saturday morning 27th May, we took the posters and planted them down the centre of the road. "Children at Play", "No Centre Parking". Nobody parked! At 10.30 a police van came, four constables and the Superintendent jumped out—and placed their own bollards "POLICE NOTICE, NO PARKING" down the centre of the road, interspersed with the People's Association posters. The police found themselves greeted with a spontaneous cheer. The action was a focal point for residents in the street. And for five weeks the action has been repeated . . . it showed that ordinary people can take action for themselves—that we can share in power. In a world of bureaucracies, authorities, "proper" procedures, that represented the assertion of initiative, independence, and choice. In a *tiny* way, it meant the conquest of powerlessness.' This type of experience can be backed many times by people living and working in such areas in our great cities; it represents the power of the neighbourhood.

Thirdly, there is the power of uninformed public opinion. I choose a negative example deliberately, for we all know of the power of informed public opinion. Not long ago the Parks Department of a certain local authority asked a vicar whether he would mind if they chopped down some trees in his churchyard on Sunday mornings (the churchyard being 'closed', and the responsibility for its upkeep having been passed onto the local authority). The vicar in question had no objection, but asked why they should want to do this on a Sunday morning rather than during the week. It transpired that such was the power of uninformed public opinion, that they were quite sure that had they cut the trees down during the week, when there were many people about, there would have been a sure and certain outcry in the local papers and petitions and the like. A spokesman said that even if a tree was rotten all the way through, the public would try to stop them destroying it, and so they preferred to work early on a Sunday morning, when public opinion was fast asleep.

A final illustration showing the existence of power where we might normally not expect to find it can be drawn from the immigrant community. The problems of immigration and of race are real enough, and I do not propose to discuss them here, but I wonder how many people realize that there is a kind of backlash power. The situation has arisen in some parts of Britain where people are so concerned not to appear to be prejudiced, that they may in fact almost be intimidated by the power of the confrontation-situation between host and immigrant communities. W. E. Hall, in the Birmingham Post of March 7th, 1968 wrote, 'The fact is that it has become extremely difficult to oppose immigration without being labelled, directly or indirectly, as a racialist. . . . Is it being racialist to say that one of the Black Power advocates, Mr. Obi Egbuna, was allowed to hold the stage in a recent television programme in a display of arrogance such as I doubt whether any television programme has tolerated before?' I write this, by the way, as one who is opposed to the recent legislation restricting immigration even further, and not as a racialist!

Institutionalized Power

So far I have been discussing the concept of power in terms of groups and of individuals, and I have tried to show that, in spite of accusations that our society is making people powerless and dehumanised, there are still many spheres of power which have yet to be fully realized. But perhaps this is not the sort of power that most people think about when they use the term. The power that probably immediately springs to mind is the power of authority. Authority, in this sense, I would see as an institutionalized expression of power. In industry everyone has power, but not everyone has it in the functional form of authority; not everyone has formal channels through which power can be exercised responsibly or creatively. Those engaged in management are entrusted with authority to exercise the power of the company in a specific way. From this position, with power vested in them, they may fulfil the functions of management in different ways. I suppose we could loosely say that there are those who manage in an authoritarian way, and those who are more disposed to a charismatic way. Authority then, is a means of transmitting power. I.C.I., for example, because of its size and its resources, etc., has tremendous power. When we ask how is this power to be used, then we are in the area of authority and management. We have

then, personal power, which is ours by reason of our being members
of a particular society; and we may have authorized power, or
delegated power, which is power vested in us by some greater,
external power.

Leadership and Authority

It is impossible to think of power, especially in major institutions like industry, without also thinking of leadership. Who
is to supply leadership? Is it reached by agreement from the
beginning, or is it usurped by tacit agreement? In industry it is
perhaps a little easier to come to grips with the leadership problem
than it is in small groups, because within industry there are
formalized channels. Having said that, though, it is common
knowledge that within the formalized channels there are struggles
for power and leadership, as there are in any group. And as any
group grows and evolves, the type of leadership needed changes,
and this is as true for the great industrial combines as it is for the
small family group.

Because of the changing character of institutions, and the
demand therefore for changing patterns of leadership, there will
always be tension between the leader and the led. In industry
this is particularly true at the foreman level, where a man is
exposed to the conflicting interests of two groups. But it should
not be thought that the conflicts and tensions of industry are only
between Management and Unions: there is often just as much
tension, and sometimes more, between one department within
management and another, between Methods and Finance, between
Works Manager and Planning. Management should not be thought
of as a homogeneous group. Thus, demarcation disputes between
Unions in a particular firm are not the only forms of in-group
fighting to be found in industry, although it perhaps says something about Britain that this is the example that always springs to
mind.

Leadership is not really so much the personal thing that we
often assume it to be. It would be perhaps more realistic if we
were to think of leadership more in functional terms. Indeed,
there are times when the concept of 'the good leader', meaning a
particular type of personality, can be dangerous, and do more
harm than good. It was Churchill who is acclaimed to have been

the great leader, and so he was in certain circumstances; but it will go down in history that it was the more insignificant Attlee who was able to lead the country into a period of tremendous social reconstruction. Thus, if leadership is more a functional thing than a personal thing, then our usual assumption that it is the designated leader who must perform this function will give way to the understanding that there are circumstances and times when other people within a group will be able to perform the function better than the designated leader. If a person other than the designated leader fulfils the function of leadership too often, then it may well be that the designated leader will find his position in peril, because a person can only exercise leadership for as long as the group allows him to, unless the institution is so entrenched that it is very difficult for the rest of the society to make its desire to express leadership felt. In such a case, the creative tension that is normal between a leader and those who are led will give way to a destructive tension, which is aimed not so much at fulfilling the objects of the group, as at ridding the group of its unwanted leader. This destructive tension is always a problem for an institution that is not flexible. The designated leader must realize that leadership does not reside in him as a person, full stop, but only in him in so far as he is designated by the group .

In plain Marxist thought, there must always be tension between those who have power and those who have not. The Maoists have tried to develop this, in order that the person with power is constantly reminded that his power is the power of the group which happens to be vested in him. They have said that army officers must serve one month a year in other ranks. Fine though this may be in theory, the army officer who becomes a private for a month, really becomes nothing more than an officer dressed as a private, for an important part of what a private is, is the knowledge that he is not an officer, and that he will not be one at the end of a month. It has about as much ultimate relevance as the Bishop who joins the Transport and General Workers' Union. This is not to condemn the system out of hand, though: it is perhaps a good thing that officers are reminded of how others live, and the Church might be more on its toes if all its Bishops belonged to a Trade Union. It is important however that we realize that the end product may not be what we originally desired.

Authority and the Church

Having said all this about leadership residing in the group, that this is functional and not personal, it is perhaps ironic that we in the Church almost deliberately tell a man at his ordination that we are making him a special kind of person. Whether or not the Church intends this, certainly a great many clergy assume that they are different, and they see the business of the laying on of hands as being the significant factor in this metamorphosis. In times past the process of ordination was a process of commissioning a man to a certain piece of work, quite often perilous in nature. More and more in today's society it is seen as offering a person security and authority. A colleague of mine was responsible for interviewing eighty ordination candidates a couple of years ago, in New Zealand. Three-quarters of them thought that they were moving into a more secure sphere of life, based upon the authority which would be conferred on them at their ordination. In one instance a man thought that by being ordained, he would *ipso facto* have more authority and power to do the same job that he was doing before. The built-in theological corrective to the power of the priesthood, that a man is exercising Christ's authority, can very easily become diabolical, and it is a short step to thinking that when the ordained man speaks, Christ speaks, therefore it behoves us to listen.

Speaking of the power and authority of Christ brings us to one of the great problems in theology today. It seems that the whole liturgical emphasis in the Church is on a concept of God which is no longer in accordance with today's outlook and understanding. Christ is portrayed as a king, and we as his subjects, but this is no constitutional monarchy: we are subjects to the total, universal, overriding authority of God. But we have moved into a social situation where such despotism, even if enlightened, is no longer tolerated. Thus, through our liturgy we are unconsciously attempting to condition people to an attitude to authority which is no longer accepted or tolerated by them. To be fair to the Church, there are parts of it trying to develop further the idea of man being a fellow-worker with God. The man on the bench in a large industrial plant can be said to be a fellow-worker with the Company Chairman, but this does not mean that the Chairman has supreme, overriding authority over him in every sphere of his life. Such a situation is no longer acceptable in today's society, and the Church is having to learn once again a new understanding of God, through its involvement in the world.

The Dilemma of Conflict

Another lesson that the Church has to learn from the world, and the sooner it does the better, is how to approach and accept the reality of conflict. It is not only the Church that is in confusion here, but the whole of our society, with its vague notions of peace and harmony. Someone said to me a year or so ago, that for our society to accept and explore conflict, would be like the Victorians accepting and exploring sex! It is to be hoped that below the surface, there is as much activity regarding conflict as there was in those days regarding sex.

Our society has taught us to see head-on collisions of ideas, ideologies, objectives and aims as something bad, something to be avoided, to be postponed at all costs. This is why when conflict has at last come into the open it has inevitably led to wars, fighting and falling out of friendship, because this destructive use is the only way that we have learned to deal with it. But if we could see conflict as a built-in part of creation, as something that we can learn to accept, a God-given gift if you like, then we would also see that it has creative uses and responses. There *are* seemingly irreconcilable differences in men, and if the only way that we can deal with them is either to let them clash violently or else withdraw from each other, then this is a sad statement about creation and the *Report from Iron Mountain*[2] would be absolutely right, and wars inevitable and necessary to our economic, social and technological development.

The Inevitability of Conflict

It is of the utmost importance then, that we accept that conflict is inevitable, and it is desirable to recognize the inevit-

[2] *Report from Iron Mountain*, ed. L. C. Lewin (Macdonald 1968), pp. 121–122:

'It is uncertain, at this time, whether peace will ever be possible. It is far more questionable, by the objective standard of continued social survival rather than that of emotional pacifism, that it were desirable even if it were demonstrably attainable. The war system, for all its subjective repugnance to important sections of 'public opinion', has demonstrated its effectiveness since the beginning of recorded history; it has provided the basis for the development of many impressively durable civilizations, including that which is dominant today. It has consistently provided unambiguous social priorities. It is, on the whole, a known quantity. A viable system of peace, assuming that the great and complex questions of substitute institutions raised in this report are both soluble and solved, would still constitute a venture into the unknown, with the inevitable risks attendant on the unforeseen, however small and however well hedged.'

ability of conflict, not as a bad thing, but as something with creative possibility, something *to be used*. Some people, agreeing with the sentiment of this argument, have nevertheless urged that instead of using the word 'conflict', we find a new 'creative' word for it. But this would be to run away from the problem. We need to use the tremendous power, energy and resources contained within the very word 'conflict', though so far the word has only prompted destructive ideas. If we are to say that the only thing we are going to recognize is tension, because this has within it, as well as the possibility of drawing apart, also the possibility of drawing together, then we are also saying that conflict is a bad thing. We may say that conflict undealt with is bad (not that conflict is bad, but that the consequences of not dealing with it are bad), but conflict recognized, accepted and dealt with is a sign of maturity. This means that the seeming irreconcilable differences that men in society may have are accepted and *contained* within that society. The existence of conflict does not have to mean that there must be an explosive eruption or the building of barriers. The mature society can say to its members that they can express their conflicts and tensions without fear of judgement, because we have learned now that the creative possibilities of this are enormous. Conflict is not to be such as something to be cured, as something wrong with society, but as an inevitable, important and integral part of life. It is perhaps worth mentioning here, that when we talk about 'containing' conflict within a society, we are not meaning 'neutralizing' conflict.

Just as in the atom electrons are held in tension, so in society it is inevitable that there should be an underlying tension. Tension between different members of a family, tension between different institutions, tensions between the leader and his people, etc. For most people, for most of the time, this is accepted without thought. 'Give and take' is a maxim which is the direct consequence of the experience of tension. Occasionally, though, this stable tension is upset by the emergence of opposing forces which seem irreconcilable. Our task is to learn how to accept this, just as we have learned to accept the fundamental tension.

Now how does this work out in industry? It is accepted that there is a fundamental tension between Management and Unions. Both, on the whole, recognize their need of the other, and whenever one becomes too strong, society at large will probably suffer.

Good management and good Unions are as necessary to each other as two good sides to make a memorable football match. But what happens when this fundamental tension is destroyed and irreconcilable differences appear? Then there is a tendency to become disillusioned about the ongoing tension. This is usually particularized, and we find one side saying that it's impossible to trust the other side, claiming that they say one thing one day and another thing the next. It is interesting that more often than not Management will claim that you cannot trust a particular Trade Unionist, whilst the Union feel a more general distrust towards the Management. In an industrial dispute, personalities become involved, and people are attacked as people rather than as functionaries of a particular viewpoint, precisely because they have not accepted that conflict is natural, that it is a built-in part of the system. When conflict is thought of as bad form, then you will get disillusion or distrust.

It would seem that wherever we find conflict, then we also find hostile, aggressive feelings. The question emerges, how are we going to deal with these? Does it inevitably mean that we must hammer the other fellow? Are there any alternatives?

A Way Forward?

Surely it should be feasible to say that if the other person feels as strongly as I do about a certain issue, then he must really feel very strongly about it indeed. Would it not be a good idea, then, to listen to what he feels about it, and thus help to create an environment where he is less afraid to hear what I have to say? How many times has the television in the capitalist West allowed the communist East freely and openly to put its case about world affairs in general? How many times has the opposite happened? I wonder if the American public would feel the same way about the war in Vietnam if ordinary communists from Asia could freely talk about their life and their outlook in America. There is also the possibility that if the Americans that you and I know could talk freely in Vietnam and the Far East, then their country would not automatically be dubbed a 'capitalistic, colonialist, warmongering nation'. I wonder what the course of history would have been if the Israelites and the Philistines had listened to each other, rather than shouted slogans to each other across the valley. Perhaps some of these examples appear extreme and unrealistic,

E

and yet isn't it true that when we are involved in a conflict situation we tend to assume that we *know* what the outcome will be? If I win it will be this, and if he wins it will be that. We all go into battle assuming that we know what Utopia is, but this we cannot know. We can say though, that if we allowed the other man to put his case, and if he allowed us to put ours, *the thing could happen.* Not his truth, nor our truth, but the evolution of a new truth, which many christians would want to call the Kingdom of Heaven. Not long ago a leader of a rather militant Union spent the weekend at a conference. He came with the feeling that he was in a foreign land, and the conference was also rather worried about how they would react to this militant. At the end of the weekend, he was expressing his gratitude to the other members for the way in which they had received him and listened to his views. He said that he had felt he was among friends. For their part, the conference felt that they had learned a tremendous amount, and the man, and his Union, was no longer seen as a threat or a problem. Between this man and this conference group *the thing* had happened. They had recognized conflict, and together they had found a new truth.

Basic to such an outlook on life is the acceptance that the society of which we are a part is an evolving society. That after any confrontation things can never be the same again. But we tend so often to work on the principle that the system we have is a static system, and will be with us for all time. We are perhaps willing to accept that technological progress will change things, but we are reluctant to accept that it is the whole of society which changes, and not merely the technological aspect. If we do believe that society is evolving though, then the most sensible thing is surely to hear what the other person has to say. I must *hear* him, no matter how hostile I feel about his hostility towards me; I allow to evolve whatever is going to be practical for us in that situation.

It is when we can look at life and society like this that the religious doctrine of original sin can be seen to make sense. Far from religion being an outdated-extra to life, and original sin being something to do with Adam and Eve, this outlook is crying out that I must realize that I am fallible, and so is my opponent. Are we prepared to say this? We may know it in our innermost being, but have we the humility to accept that a positive grasp of conflict may lead us into truths, into situations that we had not reckoned with, or do we press on arrogantly after our own ends? In international affairs, how often does a country or a leader ever admit to being wrong or mistaken? How many people are sent to war in a futile attempt to shout louder than the other person, and so make impossible the recognition of new truths? How many man hours a year are lost because both sides cling steadfastly to an ideal, a vision of Utopia, which they know will ultimately fall, as have all their other visions of Utopia?

The line that I have suggested necessitates both sides in a conflict, realizing that this can lead to something creative for them both; but very often only one side is willing to search for a new situation. The sensible man will realize that if his opponent will not talk, then there must be a reason for this, and he will devote his energies not to destroying the opponent, but to finding out why he will not talk. This may mean going right back to discovering what caused the original break in relationships. It also means that we have to be realistic about the situation. It is no good saying that we will negotiate as long as you come to the situation from a weakened position. There is no point in the Americans offering to negotiate with the North Vietnamese if they are not willing to recognize the Viet Cong. The same goes for industrial disputes. There is no point in creating an artificial position for the opponent to speak from. The new situation can only emerge from where people really are.

The Church has not set a good example in this cause. For so long the Church has paraded around the world claiming that it *knew* what the ideal was in every situation, rather than accepting the situation as it found it, and saying 'where do we go from here?'

The world is full of Utopias and of people seeking to establish them, but there is no simple answer. To hold a utopian image before a person or a society is not only a snare and a delusion, but a blatant perversion of reality, because it prevents people from ever looking at things as a whole. The problem then emerges that if we remove utopian images we are also removing the great driving forces of mankind, and if we deprive people of their Utopias, then they very quickly don't think there is anything worth fighting for.

The Christian believes that the thing which keeps us fighting in life is the attitude we have to the present situation. Love, translated into the present situation, can be the only driving force. What it will establish remains to be seen: this will be the new truth that is revealed. But this is what drives us on to be involved in the conflicts, the power struggles and tensions of society, and this is what we can contribute to them.

IV

THE USE AND ABUSE OF ORIGINAL SIN

The Rev. D. E. H. Whiteley

(1) *Introductory*

I have chosen to treat of original sin because this term covers, among other things, certain phenomena which are also of interest to sociologists, notably the pressure brought upon an individual to do something wrong because of his membership of one or more groups. I make no attempt to 'explain original sin in sociological terms', but the phenomena to which a theologian would point as evidence for original sin overlap in part with conditions which a sociologist might describe as *anomie* or as alienation. The theologian draws our attention to certain aspects of human life in picture-language drawn from Genesis: the sociologist describes some of the same phenomena in his own technical language.

In the second section I shall try to clarify the meaning of words, such as 'sin' and 'guilt', 'actual' and 'original' and to identify some of the phenomena which are of interest to sociologists and which also fall under the heading of original sin. In section (3) I shall ask what is meant by calling the concept of original sin a 'valid' concept, and in section (4) I shall expound the theology which I presuppose, for purposes of this chapter. Section (5) is devoted to a consideration of the part, large or small, which the concept of original sin plays in the lives of Christians. In the final section (6) I shall ask to what extent the concept of original sin is useful or the reverse. In trying to solve this final problem it would be useful to know the answer to certain factual questions such as whether those who hold a doctrine of original sin are in fact more able to sympathize with enemies who are not wholly to blame for all they do, since they are influenced by pressures to do wrong similar to those which afflict ourselves. On the other hand, belief in original sin may have bad consequences. It may, for example, lead to anxiety states. It is to be hoped that sociologists may be able to help at this point. I do however realize, at least in part, what a difficult request I am making. Belief in original sin, and sympathy, are subjective states which it is difficult to measure. For anxiety states referral to a doctor might act as an indicator. But even here difficulties may arise. In Britain a church-member suffering from a mild anxiety state might be less likely to go to a psychiatrist, since he might instead use the resources of his own church. In the U.S.A., I suspect, a church member might be more likely to consult a psychiatrist, since his own minister would probably see that he was referred. However, I must leave the sociologists to deal with the difficulties which lie within their proper sphere and proceed to define my terms.

(2) *Clarification of Terminology*

We must now attempt to explain the meaning of some of the words which will be used in this chapter. *Sin* differs from mere *wrong-doing* in three ways: a person who sins is to some extent *responsible* for what he does; again, he knows what he is doing and is aware that he is violating standards which he himself accepts; and, thirdly, the word 'sin' has religious, or at least quasi-religious overtones. The problem of responsibility will not be discussed here. We shall provisionally accept the 'common-sense' view that a 'normal' man who embezzles money is responsible, while a gravely disturbed psychiatric patient who tries to beat up a nurse is not. Again, I have no doubt that the middle-class man who 'fiddles' his income tax and the working-class man who helps himself to his employer's property are both doing wrong, but neither can be held to be sinning if he sincerely, though incorrectly, believes that his conduct is right. The word 'sin' normally suggests an offence against God. Atheists seldom like the word 'sin', and are unlikely to use it of themselves, precisely because of its theological overtones.

The word *guilt* describes the fact of having sinned, or the status which results from that fact. The concepts of 'sin' and 'guilt' are often confused. Indeed St. Anselm (1033–1109 A.D.) in his *Cur Deus Homo?* (*Why God became Man*) speaks of Christ's work in overcoming sin, when what he really describes is a cancellation of guilt. I personally believe that guilt, the fact of having done wrong, is of no importance at all, and that what matters is actually doing wrong. This point is important when some Christians maintain that God is unwilling or unable to help a sinner because of the barrier of guilt, which must first be overcome through the death of Christ; this is to pay attention to the legal construction called 'guilt', whereas what really matters is sin. On the other hand a *sense of guilt*, as opposed to guilt itself, is most important: a sense of guilt, whether justified by the facts or no, can have a paralysing effect upon a man and plunge him into despair.

Original sin, as suggested above, includes certain elements which might usefully be studied by sociologists. We are not *personally* responsible for original sin. Original sin must not be confused with the mere fact of finitude. A young child is naturally concerned for his own wants because he is dependent on others and not yet able to help them. Such 'infantile egotism' is not sinful, though failure to grow out of it may be a cause of sin. When Christians maintain that Jesus was 'in all points tempted like as we are, yet without sin' (Hebrews 4, 15), and that he 'advanced in wisdom and stature, and in favour with God and man' (Luke 2, 52), we mean, among other things, that he passed through the 'infantile egotism' due to human finitude without becoming sinfully selfish.

Actual sin means 'sin in so far as the agent is personally accountable for it', as opposed to original sin. *Actual guilt* is guilt arising from actual sin. It is however almost meaningless to assert that human beings are accountable for sin committed by alleged ancestors. The doctrine of original guilt is not Biblical, and hardly figures in contemporary theology. The doctrine of original sin is found only in St. Paul in the New Testament, though the whole New Testament tacitly presupposes that all men are in fact sinful.

Total depravity is a doctrine especially characteristic of Calvinists. It states that fallen man has not merely been deprived of a supernatural endowment enjoyed by Adam and Eve before the Fall. On the contrary, the whole of man's nature, including his reason and will, is distorted or *depraved*. The thrust of the doctrine is twofold. Firstly, man apart from Christ can do nothing pleasing to God. This doctrine means that all acts done by non-Christians are automatically displeasing to God. It is supported in Article XIII of the Church of England. The second thrust of the doctrine is that there is no knowledge of God apart from Christ. In this 'strong' form total depravity is, I believe, contrary both to scripture and to truth. There is, however, a 'weak' form of the doctrine of total depravity, according to which every function of man is imperfect, so that man has no infallible faculty, such as reason, conscience or insight, by which he can certainly know God. In this weak form the doctrine would appear to be true.

Original sin is traditionally held to include a turning away from God to the world, but this point will not be pursued here, since 'turning from God' is not something which can be investigated by sociological techniques. But contemporary theologians also reckon wrong-doing which is caused by community pressures to fall under the heading of original sin. For example, John Macquarrie speaks of a 'massive disorientation and perversion of human society as a whole', and adds that 'The world (Greek *kosmos*), the collective mass of mankind in its solidarity is answerable to no one, and has a hardness and irresponsibility that one rarely finds in individuals'.

This is a generally received opinion, and I am in full agreement with it, but I would wish to insist upon a qualification which I believe to be of fundamental importance. What, I would ask, do we mean in our modern pluralistic societies when we talk about *the* community or *the* 'collective mass of mankind'? I would not of course quarrel with the view that all men are involved in sin, but we do wrong to think solely of *the* community and to forget the many communities into which we are split up. Indeed, it is often in the *clash* of communities that 'original sin' is most apparent. When national communities clash in war men do deeds of which they would never have been guilty in normal circumstances. They are not free from responsibility in the same way that they would have been if they had been genuinely unaware that what they were doing would lead to death and mutilation for other human beings. On the other hand, they are not responsible in the same way as they would have been if they had done the same things as individuals under normal circumstances.

War is not the only case in which this phenomenon can be seen. What parent has not found that a child who is pleasant and easy to handle when alone becomes a devil incarnate half an hour later when he is with his 'gang'? Industrial disputes are made worse because the 'collectives' of management and labour act as the individuals composing them would never act alone. I suggest that we may with advantage use the term 'original sin' when what an individual does, though he can not disclaim responsibility for it, is due in an appreciable measure to 'community' forces. Needless to say, 'community pressure' often helps us to do better than we should otherwise have done.

We must further remember that we are none of us members of a single community, and I would suggest that the term 'original sin' may well be employed in cases where an individual belongs effectively to several communities with very different standards of behaviour. I have heard, though I cannot back my memory by reference to authorities, that immigrants from central Europe used to get into trouble in the American Middle West for stealing coal stacked in railway stations. The reason alleged was that in their home country it was accepted as justifiable in their own community, who did not regard it as stealing, to 'appropriate' firewood from the estates of the nobility, though this was not legal. Many similar examples spring to mind, such as that of the nineteenth century poacher in our own country.

But in the above cases we have two distinct and mutually exclusive sub-cultures living as part of the same state, so that the conflict was one of sub-culture against sub-culture, of poachers against squires. A different problem arises when an individual effectively belongs to two different sub-cultures with seriously conflicting standards. A few years ago it was usual to call a disturbed adolescent a 'crazy mixed-up kid'. His trouble was due, among many other things, to the fact that he was a genuine member of his family, who had one type of standard, and also of a 'gang', whose standards were entirely different, so that his standards were in fact 'mixed'. Many practical problems arise from this familiar fact. A school which tries to make its children adopt standards of honesty, responsibility, etc., which are higher than those observed at home must do so with its eyes open: is it doing more harm than good by causing an even greater split between the generations? Yet it is hardly possible for a school to condone dirtiness and unpunctuality because some of its pupils have mothers who are dirty, unpunctual or in other ways inadequate.

We must also consider changes from one community to another, and changes in the status of particular groups within a community. When a boy leaves school and goes to work in a factory, many of the moral rules and most of the religious teaching he has received are just not accepted in fact, though lip-service may be paid to some of them, by most of his work-mates. Is it surprising that he comes to reject what he has been taught as 'kids' stuff'? The difficulties experienced by immigrants are notorious, and some of the same problems arise when any transition is made from one community to another.

Another well-known difficulty arises when a group suffers a decline in prestige. The poor-white problem in the U.S.A. is a classic example. I suspect that similar pressures may provide a partial explanation for the recent rise in delinquency among the children of middle-class parents, though we need to be careful on this point since the police might bring a case to court in 1968 whereas thirty years ago, if the father was a 'solid respectable citizen', they would leave the 'criminal' to his parents. I suspect that the children of middle-class parents do not, in many cases, want to be thought of as middle-class. This is no doubt a partial reason for the appeal of the world of adolescent pop-culture, one of whose mottoes is: 'All class abandon, ye who enter here'. When an adolescent ceases to accept his inherited middle-class ideals, he may suffer from conflict, which could in itself lead to delinquency, and he may well 'opt out of the rat-race' by just failing to work and by abandoning all that is connected with respectability.

These matters are of course very familiar to sociologists. I have dwelt upon them because theologians, though well aware of the 'community' element in 'original sin', are somewhat inclined to think of 'the community' in a purely abstract fashion, instead of distinguishing the different pressures which arise, such as those between community and community, and also the tensions within an individual who effectively belongs to more than one group, as well as the trouble which arises when an individual passes from one community to another, or when a particular group suffers a decline in esteem.

I have so far written as if the symbol or model called 'original sin' could be used to designate only those forces which arise from the clash of community against community, the tensions arising when an individual belongs effectively to more than one community and the trouble which occurs when an individual or group passes from one community to another, always excepting those components which can be ascribed to the fault of the individuals involved. But we originally said that the term would be applied to 'forces leading to wrong-doing apart from those directly due to the individual agents'.

It is clear that 'original sin' has a wider sphere of reference than the 'community pressures' already mentioned. We may also apply the term original sin to, e.g., the system of chattel slavery. Some slave owners were good, and some were bad, but quite apart from individual kindness or malevolence, the system as a whole was wrong. The N.T. writers speak about being, within the system, a good slave or a good master, but they give no sign that they regard the system itself as evil, or as something which ought to be abolished. This may surprise some people in view of the fact that Paul said: 'There is no such thing as Jew and Greek, slave and freeman, male and female; for you are all one person in Jesus Christ' (Gal. iii. 28). I would suggest two reasons. First, the fact that there is no 'male and female' means that Paul is not speaking about the whole of normal life in this world, but about part of it, namely the relation to Christ. Secondly, the Christians in the apostolic period believed that the world would soon end, so far-reaching programmes of social reform, if only for this reason, were outside their field of vision. In the same way, the subjection of women may be regarded as part of the content of original sin where there is real subjection and the women are oppressed. Among traditional Jews, for example, women seem to an outsider to be 'subjected', but it is probably true that they are so much mistresses within the home that they are not really oppressed.

To come to our own western civilization, it might be held that distribution smacks of original sin. Much effort has to be 'wasted' in advertising which might be better used in reducing prices. Again, the press rely for their revenue very largely upon advertising revenue, which makes it all the more important to increase circulation at all costs. It naturally follows that the popular press has become almost a branch of the entertainment industry. The truth is often suppressed because financial considerations demand that the readers shall be told what the readers want to hear. Anyone who works in advertising or the press will protest that my strictures are unfair. Quite so: they *are* unfair if the blame is placed solely on the individuals concerned. In fact the trouble is due not so much to the individuals as to the financial and other pressures under which they have to work. That is precisely why I include them under the term 'original sin'.

I would also use the term 'original sin' when, e.g., a window-cleaner has to pay 'protection-money' to a gangster as the price of working in a particular locality. It is true that a heroic window-cleaner might move away or court trouble by informing the police. But few members of the human race are heroes. I feel justified in speaking of original sin when outside pressures are such that the normal man cannot reasonably be expected to stand up against them. It might be suggested that the term should also be used for pressures which drive people in the direction of addiction to alcohol or to other drugs. I should personally use the language of the 'demonic' in cases where individuals are as it were picked out of a community as opposed to cases where an entire group is involved. Thus press employees are all under the pressure of original sin for reasons mentioned above, and some of them fall victims to the 'demon rum'. 'Original sin' has traditionally been used for what is universally pervasive in one form or another, though it may affect different groups in different ways. 'Demon' language has been used for evils that are less generally pervasive. Clearly there can be an overlap in the referend: that is, some may use 'demon' language about phenomena to which others would apply the term 'original sin'. It is of course a commonplace of the history of doctrines that in Jewish thought the origin of sin and evil was ascribed sometimes to Adam and/or Eve, sometimes to 'Fallen angels', which virtually means demons, and sometimes to the 'evil impulse'.

Now the Fall and demons have this in common. They are models, but they are mythological in a sense in which the models used by the physical scientist are not. By being mythological they lose in precision and in acceptability to many people. It is argued in their favour that they are more acceptable to other people, and that they can function at a subconscious level in a way which would not be possible for those models which are not mythological.

A further point worthy of note is that the mythological model employed to represent original sin is that of a *Fall*, that is, a Fall *from* something. This model is compatible with the conviction that at one time in the past original sin did not exist, and this further makes it easy to believe that the time will come again when original sin will no longer exist: we are living in a temporary period of evil, a period between the Fall of Man and the Second Coming of Jesus Christ. It is clear that we are not dealing with a tightly bound system in which one proposition can be strictly deduced from others. We are dealing with a complex of convictions expressed by means of mythological models which are mutually compatible, but which cannot be deduced from each other. Perhaps it is necessary for me to add once more that although I speak of mythological models I believe that through them we are made aware of something real.

(3) *The Validity of the Concept of Original Sin*

A hundred years ago adherents of popular Christianity would have said that the concept of Original Sin was valid in the sense that a finite time after the creation of the world, which occurred at 9 a.m. on October 9th, 4004 B.C., the events recorded in Genesis iii took place and that, as a result, all human being are liable to death and sinful (original sin). In addition all human beings are accountable for what Adam and Eve did (original guilt). Dr. Billy Graham, to judge from a sermon I heard him preach in Oxford some years ago, still believes both in original sin and in original guilt. But hardly any English clergy of whatever denomination would agree with him, nor would the bulk of the laity. Even the conservative evangelicals, who accept the inerrancy of scripture, frequently have reservations about the literal historicity of the early chapters of Genesis.

Most theologians in fact believe that the creation and fall were not successive events in time but that they are 'parables' or models pointing to things which have always been true about human beings and will be as long as we continue to inhabit this planet. Original sin is not an *explanation* of our state of sinfulness but a partial characterization of it. It suggests that our sinfulness includes 'having a blind eye turned towards God' and certain 'community pressures' which force us into sin. We shall in the main confine our attention to the 'community pressures' because they lie on the frontier between sociology and theology, although the Godward aspect is a vital part of any Christian view of sin.

It is pointless to ask if the doctrine of original sin as regards 'community pressures' is true or false. In that it refers to facts it is clearly true, or, to be more precise, one way of representing the truth, just as the 'wave-theory' is one model for representing the phenomena we observe in the study of light, and the 'corpuscular theory' another. It is more suitable to ask whether 'original sin' is a useful model for handling the phenomena and whether, and if so on what occasions, it is more 'useful' than the entirely different concepts which a sociologist would normally employ in studying the very same phenomena. In order to answer the question whether the concept of original sin is a 'good' model we must first ask how the model is actually used by Christians in theology, in preaching, in worship, in art and in private prayer and meditation. But there is something else which must be done before we even begin to examine how the concept of original sin is employed. When we say of something that it is good or bad or useful, we are tacitly pre-supposing some standard by which we judge it. I must now make clear my own theological presuppositions so far as they underlie and affect my treatment of the subject of this chapter.

(4) *The Theological Presuppositions of this Chapter*

For purposes of this chapter I regard the following as presuppositions, though I should of course be ready to argue in favour of these beliefs elsewhere.

The word 'God' is not 'meaningless', and it does not convey information *only* about my own feelings, attitudes and policy with regard to life. It conveys information about a reality I believe in. It is because I believe in this reality that I feel as I do and that my attitudes and 'policy towards life' are what they are. This 'reality' which I call 'God' cannot be described directly, in the way that a table can be described directly as 'brown'. God's characteristics can be hinted at only indirectly by means of such 'models' as 'Father', 'Up there', 'Ground of our being' and 'Love'. All these models are useful to the science of theology in 'hinting' at the nature of God. Of course, some of them may for understandable reasons be less helpful psychologically to some people than to others. Bishop Robinson finds 'up there' and 'out there' unhelpful models. His feelings are shared by many, but not by all. What matters at this point is to recognize that the usefulness of models depends upon the intellectual and psychological background of those it is desired to communicate with, and therefore may vary to a considerable extent between one individual and another or between one group and another.

God's purpose for human beings living on this planet is that they should live together, strive against each other and with their environment and so develop into beings capable of loving God and each other. For the sake of completeness I must add that I think this process continues after death, though I do not see how this affects our present discussion. Such a belief about the purpose of human life fits in with the belief that God is love, or rather that 'love' is a revealing model to apply to God, though it cannot be strictly deduced from it.

Since we are living in a material world it is natural that there should be an unawareness of God, and since it is part of God's purpose that we should grow as persons, that is, as members of communities, it is natural and inevitable that we should be subject to community pressures which impel us in the direction of collective selfishness. Such pressures are inevitable if we are to grow together towards love, and are necessary for our personal and social health, just as blood-pressure is necessary for our physical health, since without it the body would not be supplied with a constant stream of blood. But if the blood-pressure becomes too high—and only a medical practitioner can draw the line between what is and is not excessive—then it constitutes a serious danger to health. In particular, too high a blood-pressure may damage the kidneys. But it is one of the functions of the kidneys to regulate the blood-pressure, so when the kidneys are damaged the blood-pressure again increases. As a result the patient, for that is what he has now become, is launched upon a rapidly descending spiral until his life is terminated by, e.g., a stroke. All this happens because blood-pressure, which is necessary and desirable, has become too great for the needs of the body as a whole. It is obvious that there are clear parallels in the moral life of communities and individuals, as will appear later.

God's attitude to this can be hinted at if we employ the model of a doctor. A doctor does not try to 'cure' normal blood-pressure or normal blood-clotting: he takes action only when the blood-pressure is too high or the blood's clotting power increases so that thrombosis is likely to occur. In the same way, God is not 'against' normal community loyalties, normal sexuality, or a normal desire to 'get on' but only against dangerous departures from normality. Above all, a doctor does not refuse to help a patient because he is ill. Nor does God require to be propitiated because of our sin. He is concerned only that we should overcome it.

Original sin is of course a symbol or model. It is not to be identified exclusively with any event in history or in prehistory, though it symbolizes realities which pervade all history. On the other hand, the life, death and resurrection of Christ are facts of history, but in addition to being historical facts they represent and 'symbolize' and indeed 'mediate' such realities, including the power and love of God. It has been necessary to include this paragraph in order to make my position clear, and I shall not develop any of the points further since they do not directly affect the social sciences.

Two points arise so directly out of this thumb-nail sketch of basic theology that I shall deal with them at once. Though in fact all humans are sinful, it is not a sin to be human. It is impossible to be human in any normal sense without belonging to groups such as family, neighbourhood groups, class or nation. No one kind of group is universal: a child may grow up either in a Western household-family, or in an African extended family, or in an Israeli *kibbutz*, but in each case he belongs to a group. Group loyalty is good and natural and a necessary condition of human development. It is no more to be condemned than normal blood-pressure. But just as excessive blood-pressure can damage the kidneys, with the result that kidney damage induces even higher blood-pressure, so that a descending spiral results, excessive loyalty to a community can cause hostility by other communities. In the U.S.A. neglect of the negroes has led to an excessive loyalty to the negro cause in the case of the Black Muslims. This may lead white Americans to become afraid and to take harsh measures which could lead to an analogous descending spiral. When such race hatred arises individual blacks and whites do things they that would not do as individuals apart from the abnormal community situation. This is a set of circumstances which can fairly be referred to 'original sin'.

The connexion between original sin and sexuality is one which has been made too lightly in the past. Sexuality, as such, is neither evil nor sinful. It has sometimes been imagined that it is, partly because of the words of Christ: 'But I say to you that every one who looks at a woman lustfully has already committed adultery with her in his heart' (Matt. V, 28). Christ meant simply that feeling of desire for a woman to whom he is not married or at any rate not yet married is something every normal male experiences, and is not sinful or a proof of original sin. Sin arises if the man goes on to actual fornication or adultery, or if he dwells too much on such thoughts. In the latter case it is not easy to draw the line. In the case of fornication and adultery what is wrong is not the sexuality as such, but the irresponsibility of the act and the fact that the woman is being treated impersonally: in other words, the sheer lack of love, even though the man may be in one sense 'in love' with her.

(5) *The Place of the Concept of 'Original Sin' in the life of Christians*

In this section I am mainly concerned to ask the purely factual question, what part does the concept of original sin play in the life of the Christian? Unfortunately my approach must be intuitive and anecdotal. I should welcome further evidence from sociologists.

First, how does a theological concept such as original sin play a part in the life of Christians at all? It clearly plays a large part in the thinking of theologians and of the Christian intelligentsia, and in our next section we shall consider the extent to which this model is employed usefully or the reverse.

But what of the unreflecting majority? It might be argued that it plays a large part in the lives of more than 50 per cent of the population of the country, since original sin is presupposed by the practice of Infant Baptism. But I suspect that Infant Baptism for the majority who bring their children to be baptized is a detached custom, no longer vitally connected with the theological doctrine of original sin, although the doctrine and the practice formerly supported each other and were inseparably connected. Would it be possible by existing techniques to determine the extent to which surviving religious practices are evidence for the survival of the beliefs with which at one time they were integrally involved?

Original sin plays a part in liturgy, in hymns, and to some extent in Christian poetry and plastic art. Because it is a vivid, concrete symbol as expressed in the story of Adam and Eve in Genesis iii it can play a part in the 'subconscious', to use an outmoded expression for which I do not know the modern equivalent. Because Adam is a person, we can 'identify' with him. In Cardinal Newman's lines:

> O loving wisdom of our God!
>   When all was sin and shame,
> A second Adam to the fight
> And to the rescue came.

F

O wisest love! that flesh and blood,
   Which did in Adam fail,
Should strive afresh against their foe,
   Should strive and should prevail.

O generous love! that he who smote
   In man for man the foe,
The double agony in Man
   For man should undergo.

We are invited to identify both with Adam and with Christ, that is, to accept the fact of the almost unlimited extent of evil and the fact that we are involved in evil greater than anything due to our own limited sin, and *nevertheless* to identify with a power beyond ourselves yet intimately involved with us and capable of finally overcoming all the evil and sin. Such identification should be powerful medicine indeed even if it were only a comforting illusion, still more if it points at the actual truth by means of models which have emotional overtones and can therefore affect our feeling and action.

This suggests a possible line of enquiry. The 'myth' of a Fall is widespread. We should like to know the proportion of those members of the population of Great Britain to whom the idea of a Fall is actually or potentially a stirring symbol. Again, is this a symbol of power in all humans, or only among those who have been subjected to certain cultural pressures? I should naturally guess that the latter alternative is correct. But further points arise. The idea of a Fall is not peculiar to Christianity. It would appear to have a place in classical Marxism. But Marxism arose within populations influenced by the Judaeo-Christian tradition. Does the symbol retain its power in a community which has lost its roots in the neolithic past and is now purely 'industrial' in outlook? Many of the Japanese are both industrialized and secularized in spite of formal observances surviving from Buddhism and Shintoism. We should like to know if a realization of original sin is universal in 'the human situation' or whether it is found in certain cultural environments only. It is of course an over-simplification to speak of all cultures as either 'shame cultures' or 'guilt cultures' in an exclusive sense. It would however be interesting to know whether the ideas of a Fall and ideas of the 'original sin' type are more prevalent or more deeply rooted in what may be described as predominantly a guilt culture than they are in a community which has predominantly a shame culture. Further it would be of interest to know how widely this realization of original sin is symbolized by means of the concept of a Fall.

At this point a distinction of major importance must be made. The average man or woman is only too well aware that 'something always goes wrong', that there is a force of evil in the world. Sometimes this is identified with 'the employers' or 'the Trade Unions', sometimes it is a mere 'they'. Further, there is a wide-spread feeling that we are not able to deal effectively with our problems. People say that it is due to their 'glands', but the endocrine glands are here being used mythologically to represent a weight of evil which is not properly understood. Now I would not identify this vaguely conceived force of evil with 'original sin'. At the level of twelve-year-old physics, the mass of a body can be correlated with weight if and only if the body in question is con-sidered in relation to another body such as the earth, in which case the body concerned has 'weight' which is a measure of the gravitational force exercised upon it by the earth. Mass is analog-ous to 'generalized evil', and weight to 'generalized evil considered in relation to God'. My contention that the distinction between 'generalized evil' and original sin is important may be expressed in another way: it makes a difference whether or no the concept is entertained by itself or within the framework of a theistic or Christian belief. In the latter case, the way is readily open for the further belief that the evil can and eventually will be overcome, though this is beyond the power of the individuals concerned.

'Generalized evil' would seem a fit description for what we find in many contemporary writings, such as those of Camus, and in a high proportion of the songs which gain a place in the 'top twenty'. I may add that a half-acknowledged interest in astrology would seem to be more widespread now than it was at the begin-ning of the century. Is this due in part to a desire at least to view 'general evil' and 'fate' as part of a comprehensible system now that 'evil' is no longer placed within a theistic framework as symbol-ized by the concept 'original sin'?

(6) Is the Concept 'Original Sin' Useful?

In the previous section we tried to indicate the part played by the concept of original sin in the lives of Christians. It might be more accurate to say that we tried to indicate the need for a proper enquiry to be undertaken. We must now ask whether the concept of original sin, where it is employed, is useful or the reverse. To anticipate, it may be said in general terms that it can play a useful part, for some people, at the emotional level in worship, prayer, etc., provided that it is kept firmly within a theistic framework, which means that we keep in view the possibility of overcoming it, and do not merely acknowledge its existence. At the intellectual level, the concept of original sin is of value when employed as a warning, provided that it is not allowed to stand in the way of closer analysis by means of other concepts which have greater precision but less emotive power.

If we allow our feelings to be influenced by the concept of original sin, we *ought* not to 'contract out' of situations. We are involved in evil situations by the mere fact that we are human: even if we are not personally accountable for much of the evil in the world, we have a responsibility to do something about it. Again, we *ought* to feel that our enemies are not solely and personally responsible for the evil we suffer at their hands, but *should* realize that they are partly the victims of pressures which beat upon us also, and fellow-sufferers with ourselves in the general evil which afflicts the human race.

Again, those who are influenced by the concept of original sin *ought* not to be surprised or discouraged when they overcome one evil only to find that another has arisen. It is a common-place that slum clearance solves some problems and raises others by breaking up 'extended families' and causing increased loneliness. Those whose minds are influenced by the concept of original sin *ought* to expect and anticipate further difficulties and not allow themselves to be put off. They *ought* to consider the problem as a whole and to undertake e.g. slum clearance if it seems on balance desirable.

In the last two paragraphs I have said that those who are influenced by the concept of original sin *ought* to be helped by it in three ways. They *ought* to acknowledge their responsibility to assist in overcoming evil for which they are not personally accountable, to refrain from blaming their enemies as if they were personally responsible for all that they may have done, and to accept without dismay the fact that the solution of one problem frequently creates others. In each case the word 'ought' has been placed in italics, since one might naturally suppose that belief in original sin would have these effects. But does belief in original sin actually produce these effects? Further, the result may depend upon how original sin is presented. It is difficult to measure anything so subjective as belief in original sin, and it is also difficult to measure the desirable characteristics which this belief ought to induce. If it is possible to discover whether there is in fact a significant positive correlation between belief in original sin and these desirable characteristics the interest is not merely academic. In particular, clergy would like to know how to present this doctrine, within the total framework of Christian teaching, in such a way that these benefits do in fact ensue.

We must now turn to the other side of the coin, which is equally hard to examine, and for similar reasons. If a man is influenced by the concept of orginal sin, he may be liable to certain undesirable characteristics. He may, firstly, be so overwhelmed by the gravity of original sin that he lies down under the burden and makes no effort to face his problems. This is what we should expect above all if the belief in original sin is stronger, or carries more powerful emotional overtones than the belief in God. We might also expect a failure to face practical problems if the person concerned further believes that the world as such is evil. The orthodox belief that God created the world, and that human flesh, that is, a complete human personality, was 'assumed' by the Second Person of the Trinity in the Incarnation is normally treated in sermons to suggest that the world is not basically evil, but that in spite of original sin it is still God's world and a sphere in which we can and should do God's will and face our problems.

The weakness mentioned in the last paragraph is one of moral feebleness. This may be a result of belief in original sin, or it may be that a man who is morally feeble for other reasons, and who lives in a Christian environment where the idea of original sin is 'in the air', adopts it with fervour as a rationalization of and an excuse for his moral feebleness. In the same way there may be a connexion between on the one hand a belief in original sin, and on the other hand a repulsive amalgam of self-protective arrogance and intellectual laziness. I imagine we have most of us met the man who when faced with a difficult situation such as the colour problem or the generation-split says with an air of triumph: 'It's all a matter of original sin', as if this were a profound intellectual discovery, and goes on to say that all the sociologists, psychologists and criminologists in the world can torture their brains in vain without finding a solution. These two abuses springing from a belief in original sin, moral feebleness and an arrogant intellectual laziness (assuming that belief in original sin is, at least in some cases, the cause and not a rationalization of the abuse) are due to a failure to keep belief in original sin firmly in its right place within the complete framework of Christian doctrine. If 'corrected' by a proper belief in the doctrine that man is made in the image of God and in the doctrine of God's redemption, then belief in original sin should not lead either to moral feebleness or to intellectual laziness.

I have spoken about the good and evil which may result from a belief in original sin. I now wish to raise a problem. Does teaching and preaching about original sin cause people to have a sense of guilt which they would otherwise lack? On the other hand, does the symbol 'original sin' crystallize dimly realized feelings of being involved in communal guilt which could not otherwise have been given articulate expression? It might be possible to answer this question by examining sects who lay stress on original sin, always provided that we can find a proper control, that is other people who do not share the religious beliefs of the group being studied, but are similar in all other relevant respects. It might be possible to compare two sects, both of which had a similar sense of separateness from the community at large, and a similar economic and social background. If one sect had a strong belief in original sin and the other did not, then a difference between e.g. the incidence of mental breakdown between the two groups might be significant. I suspect that a moderate emphasis upon sin, both actual and original, accompanied by a balancing upon redemption and grace might have a therapeutic effect.

I wish to make one final point. Theologians when they talk of sin are in danger of projecting their own feelings, and condemning in others what they fear in themselves. A factual check by means of sociological investigation may help to save theologians from this danger. The sociologist has a different professional temptation. Because human life can be analysed in conceptual terms, he may lose sight of the fact that persons are persons. He may be saved from this danger by considering how the theologian examines some of the same phenomena by means of picture language which is perhaps less clear, but does not obscure the sense of mystery.

V

THE OVERCOMING OF ALIENATION

THE REV. F. W. DILLISTONE

i

The Times of March 7th, 1968, gave prominence to an article by Des Wilson, Director of *Shelter*, entitled 'Why youth bitterly rebels against *"the system"*.' It spoke of unrest, frustration and a spirit of rebellion among our educated young people. It declared that Parliament had brought itself close to 'complete alienation' from the nation's youth. It concluded that this estrangement is 'about to lead to a rebellion by youth that will be more bitter and more effective than anything yet experienced'.

When the article went on to ask what it is against which young people are rebelling it defined the real enemy as *the system*. Not the older generation, not the rulers in themselves, not a particular section of society, but *the system*. This term, it seemed, defied too close analysis. It is 'everything that holds up progress' (in point of fact 'progress' is a very question-begging term): it is the 'mental application of bureaucracy' (again what does 'bureaucracy' really mean?): 'it is people in key positions who refuse to listen to the urgent voice of change. It is everybody waiting for their turn, and the person at the front staying there too long'.

So after all the alienation is from *persons*—persons who resist change, cling to position and privilege, put obstacles in the way of youth pressing forward to an undefined goal. Presumably such persons can be found in all ranks of life. But it is obvious that the place where they are most likely to be found is in centres of *government*, whether the government be political or civic or ecclesiastical or educational or industrial. If the concept of government be allowed at all, then the governors must govern: and this implies the upholding of certain steady patterns of behaviour. It is true that steady patterns are more difficult to frame today than ever before and the temptation is for governors everywhere to panic, to dig in their heels and say 'Thus far and no farther'! Yet government there must be unless life is to become utterly chaotic and anarchic. What the world is looking for everywhere is a system in which steadiness includes constant change, patterns are unlimitedly flexible and goals are attained through the exercise of maximum sensitivity. And it is striking that such systems are playing increasingly important parts in the realms of mathematics and engineering. But for the present, alienation remains the dominant mood.[1]

Robert A. Nisbet, when preparing a fresh edition of his book *The Quest for Community*, wrote a new preface in which he reflected on some of the changes which had taken place in the decade since 1952 when the book first appeared. 'It has become steadily clearer to me', he writes, 'that alienation is one of the determining realities of the contemporary age: not merely a key concept for philosophy, literature and the social sciences (making obsolete or irrelevant many of the rationalistic premises descended from the Enlightenment) but a cultural and psychological condition implicating ever larger sections of the population'.

'By alienation I mean the state of mind that can find a social order remote, incomprehensible, or fraudulent; beyond real hope or desire: inviting apathy, boredom or even hostility. The individual not only does not feel a part of the social order: he has lost interest in being a part of it. For a constantly enlarging number of persons, including, significantly, young persons of high school and college age, this state of alienation has become profoundly influential in both behaviour and thought. Not all the manufactured symbols of togetherness, the ever-ready programmes of human relations, patio festivals in suburbia and our quadrennial crusades for presidential candidates hide the fact that for millions of persons such institutions as state, political party, business, church, labour union and even family have become remote and increasingly difficult to give any part of one's self to'.

If this was already clear to Nisbet at the beginning of the '60s, it is surely even more apparent as we approach the end. And here I quote from a more recent book by Herbert Read. In the Preface to *Art and Alienation* he writes: 'Never before in the history of our Western world has the divorce between man and nature, between man and his fellow men, between individual man and his "self-hood" been so complete. Such is one of the main effects of that system of production we call capitalism, as Marx foresaw. We now realise that not capitalism alone, but the whole character and

---

[1] For a full analysis I refer to Dr. Martin's opening essay in this volume.

scope of a technological civilization is involved (the end of capitaliz-ation in certain countries has not meant the end of alienation). To change the world, meaning the prevailing economic system, is not enough. The fragmented psyche must be reconstituted, and only the creative therapy we call art offers that possibility'.

ii

From these two quotations I want to extract certain interesting common convictions. The first is that the sense of alienation which in certain respects has always been characteristic of human life has reached a degree of intensity and universality in the period since the Second World War such as has never been known before. Many factors have doubtless operated in bringing this about. One of the most powerful has been the rapid extension of the media of human inter-communication. But of the existence of this widespread feeling there can hardly be serious question.

The second, and this is more important, is that alienation has to be regarded not simply as a separation between man and his neighbour, man and his work—unless there can be a certain 'distancing' in all human relations there can be no growth to maturity—but as a dividedness within man's own self, as a psychic disruption. Nisbet emphasizes a state of mind, a feeling, an interest: Read emphasizes 'feelings of anxiety and despair, of rootlessness and insecurity, of isolation and apathy', a fragmentation of the whole psyche, and he quotes a key passage from Erich Fromm which speaks of the alienated person as being 'out of touch with himself as he is out of touch with any other person'. Indeed I gain the impression from all these writings that we have reached a stage when the outward structures within which man lives are no longer regarded as the most serious source of the unrest and frustration which are so evident in the world of humanity. Even if these conditions could be altered and radically changed over-night would this necessarily remove the sense of alienation? There seems to be a growing disillusionment about what can be done by manipulating the structures of politics and economics. The wound in the psyche remains. How can healing be found?[2]

[2] Cp. Eugène Ionesco in *Fragments of a Journal:* 'I am limited and alienated, others are limited and alienated, and all forms of action, of revolution, of literature are only ways of forgetting alienation for a moment, not remedies for alienation. The end of it all can only be an even more lucid, hence more desperate, awakening. A vast weariness overwhelms me: presumably psycho-logical in origin, with no apparent cause, but the cause of which I know: the certain, or almost certain, knowledge, that all is vanity.'

Let me say at once that I do not advocate and I do not think that any of these authors would advocate a policy of despair or an attitude of 'couldn't-t-care-less' towards these regulating structures of social life. Quite clearly there has to be organization for the production and distribution of life's necessities and if this is not done according to some system it will ultimately be done by the dominating will of a dictator. There can be no withdrawal from the effort to discover a better system of political and economic structures.

Yet if the vast changes in man's external framework over the past century have indeed caused him to become more and more alienated from his environment and more and more divided within his own inner self, are there ways by which the self can gain a fuller integration, can experience a certain healing or wholeness, even while the outward world of phenomena seems so alien, so meaningless, so impersonal? Presumably the chief claims to provide ways of healing and recovery have come from the psychotherapist, the minister of religion and the artist. I propose to glance at each of these claims in turn.

iii

A very frank examination of the first is to be found in the collection of essays entitled *Psychoanalysis Observed*. It is hard for a layman to pass judgement on such a book, but at least he lays it down with the sense that the psychotherapist today is dissatisfied with what has so far been achieved by orthodox psychoanalytical methods and is modest in his claims about what constitutes a 'cure'. Indeed Anthony Storr in his essay 'The Concept of Cure' grapples earnestly with the question of how we are to give any satisfactory interpretation to such a phrase as psychological *health*. Not, he urges, by analogies drawn from the cure of physical disease. The matter is far more complex, far more tentative. The psychotherapist cannot use the knife and only gradually is he learning the effect of drugs. Yet it can at least be said that steps towards a cure, towards a closer integration of the personality, have come through the relationship of doctor and patient, a relationship which is essentially one of patience, understanding, and acceptance. Verbal communications are encouraged and assistance is given in the task of interpretation. A new framework of reference is gradually established in which the patient may begin to make connections for himself and to see how his own condition can be explained. Emotional integration can begin by the building up of a relationship with at least *one* other—the therapist himself. There is little possibility of *sudden* cure but a process of healing can in many cases be initiated.

I have no competence to assess the results of psychotherapy, but from the point of view of the interested spectator two factors appear to be of supreme importance. The first is the establishment of a *free flow* between two centres of personal life. There is a blockage somewhere, a barrier to free communication and this constitutes a state of alienation. By whatever means, the free flow must be restored. But this in itself is not enough. There must also be the establishment of *an image of wholeness*. The patient's condition is one of disconnectedness. There are innumerable bits and pieces which possess no pattern of integration. Somehow what is remembered from early life, what is recalled from dreams, what pours out spontaneously when blocks are removed, must be brought within the ambit of a possible image of wholeness.[3] How the contours of this image are to be defined is, I realize, a matter of extreme difficulty and of continuing debate. But I want only to record the impression of an outsider that unless the free flow can be initiated and the integrating image established, the process of healing can hardly be said to have begun.

iv

I turn to the minister of religion. Normally he assumes that the religious faith and practice to which he is himself committed can be a powerful agent in bringing salvation to those who are in some way in a state of weakness or bondage or hopelessness. He has often used the word sin but might just as well have used the word alienation or the term estrangement. No theologian that I know has applied these latter terms more comprehensively to man's condition that has Paul Tillich. He speaks of man as being alienated or estranged from his world, from his neighbour, from himself, from the ground of his being. It is not just the sick man, the abnormal man who is so alienated. This is a universal condition which calls for a universal remedy.

[3] 'Shape, pattern, growth, rhythm, interlocking parts of whatever kind, restore ourselves to ourselves,' Adrian Stokes, *Greek Culture and the Ego* (Tavistock, 1958), p. 52.

The word translated 'alienated' in the Authorised Version of the Bible occurs only three times in the New Testament but it is an appropriate term to use in our present context since its root concern is with '*otherness*'. And it is inferred that the root condition of man himself is that of *otherness* or alienation. In contrast the word which in the New Testament is used for the healing process and which in our English version is translated as 'reconciliation', literally means *downing the otherness*. The otherness is in some way downed or diminished or destroyed. This is the term Tillich uses for the whole process by which man's universal alienation is overcome.

But how in point of fact is it worked out? How does this *reconciliation* begin to come to pass? Interestingly the two factors which I have already pin-pointed in the field of psychotherapy prove to be of outstanding significance in Tillich's own exposition. In the first place he insists upon the importance of the healing *relationship*. 'You cannot help people,' he says, 'by telling them what to do. You can help them only by giving them something —by accepting them. This means help through the grace which is active in the healing relationship whether it is done by the minister or by the doctor. This, of course, includes the Reformation point of view, namely, you must feel that you have been accepted. Only then can one accept himself. It is never the other way around. That was the plight of Luther in his struggle against the distorted late Roman Church which wanted 'that men make themselves first acceptable and then God would accept them'. But it is always the other way around. 'First you must be accepted. Then you can accept yourself, and that means, you can be healed'.

Secondly there is the question of the integrating pattern. Here Tillich is quite explicit. One of the key-concepts of this total theological system is 'the picture of the New Being in Jesus the Christ'. So he affirms that in the New Testament picture of the Christ we are given an image of the New Reality 'which makes the fulfilment of our essential being possible'. 'Christ,' he writes, 'is the place where the New Reality is completely manifest because in him in every moment, the anxiety of finitude and the existential conflicts are overcome. This means that he is not another law. What he is, is healing power overcoming estrangement because he himself was not estranged.'

I realize that these are but the bare bones of a theological system and that much needs to be expounded in more detail. But

I am only concerned at the moment to draw attention to the exposition of a way of reconciliation by a profoundly *religious* man. In his view the establishment of a free flow (full *acceptance*) within a healing relationship and the presentation of an *integrating image* (the New Being in Jesus the Christ) for the sinner's contemplation are the all-important matters in the overcoming of alienation.

V

Finally I am deeply interested in the contribution of the artist. He perhaps is more vividly aware of 'alienation' or 'otherness' than is the case with any other member of the community. He is often overpowered by the impact of what he sees with his eyes, hears with his ears, feels on his pulses: yet he is constantly gripped by the inner image, the inner rhythm, the inner feeling arising within his own consciousness or maybe out of the unconscious. How are outward phenomena and inward feelings to be reconciled?

In unfolding the general theme of *alienation* Herbert Read uses the striking phrase 'the atrophy of sensibility'. This he believes is the most sinister aspect of modern civilization. It has come about through the 'progressive divorce of human faculties from natural processes'. 'If seeing and handling, touching and learning and all the refinements of sensation that developed historically in the conquest of nature and the manipulation of material substances are not educed and trained from birth to maturity the result is a being that hardly deserves to be called human: a dull-eyed, bored and listless automaton whose one desire is for violence in some form or other—violent action, violent sounds, distractions of any kind', that can penetrate to its deadened nerves. This for Read is alienation—the man with sensibilities atrophied confronting a world which he regards only as raw material for quantifying, manipulating and utilising. The extreme is reached when fellow human beings are no longer regarded as flesh and blood, as spirit and person, but as objects and things, as fodder for the machine and as fuel for the flames.

If such a state of alienation does in fact exist, what is Read's proposed remedy? It is what in the widest sense he has called Education through Art. But he interprets this in no narrow sense. In the first place he is concerned with what I have previously called the restoration of *free flow*. He refers to China which in its best days has insisted that no education is complete which does not include 'some direct contact with nature'. 'Such a policy takes the citizen back to the point where civilization is born, and heals the wound which we have called alienation. If such a policy succeeds in reuniting the divided psyche of man, *a vital energy will once more begin to flow from sensation to feeling, from imagination to mind* (my italics). But as things are at present, this precious stream will remain at the mercy of ideologists, to be dammed and diverted to the fulfilment of their materialistic aims.'

Secondly, he insists upon the power of the image as it is created by the man of genius. This is the contribution of the particular artist for there is no absolute democratization or equalization in art. 'The artist, whether he is a poet or a painter, a musician or a potter, "gives concrete shape to sensations and perceptions" (Cézanne) and what he manifests is *this* shape, in colours, in words, in sounds.' And it is by such a manifested shape or image that stirrings of new life are stimulated. Through such images the fragmentation of consciousness can receive nodal integrations and presumably (though Read does not say this) expand to an ever fuller integration of life through a progressive reconciliation of its alienations.

vi

In the latter half of his book Read gives particular examples of the general principles which he has enunciated in the first part. Of these I find the chapter on the work of Henry Moore specially interesting and illuminating. Moore's art has at all times been more related to vitality than to what is generally called beauty. Such a division cannot, I think, be pressed too far but in art there is undoubtedly a division of emphasis between that which draws the imagination towards wholeness, peace, beauty, grace, proportion, harmony and that which produces the sense of tension, vitality, conflict, even tragedy: the two need not be finally unreconcilable but it is likely that a particular artist will tend in one direction or the other.

In Moore's work it is the second of those emphases that is paramount and only occasionally can the first be *sensed*. But if we think of his art as a tremendous re-manifestation of vitality, undoubtedly gained by feeling his way back to the *beginnings* in every sense of that term, how in actual fact does it take shape? As Read clearly shows, he has been virtually obsessed by two concrete images—the Mother and Child on the one hand, the Reclining Figure on the other. And I do not think it would be an over-simplification to see these as concerned on the one hand with the most influential of all human relationships and on the other with the basic image of all creative life. To enter with sympathy into the deepest feeling expressed through these images is to be restored to a *free flow* of affection which in its highest form we call *love* and to be re-committed to that *integrating image* which in its highest form we call the image of *sacrifice*.

Commenting on the Mother and Child motif Read writes: 'The mother as idealised becomes the Great Mother, the goddess of human fertility or fecundity; the Child is the symbol of genetic promise and continuity, of life renewed in each generation. . . . It would be a mistake, however, to assume that Moore's approach to the subject is in any way systematic or ideological. Rather it is essentially human, and is not in need of an intellectual justification. It explores every direct aspect of the personal relationship—the instinctive dependence of the sucking child; the child clinging to the mother for protection; the child looking outward to assert its independence; the aggressive child, renouncing the breasts that feed it; and finally the child reconciled in the unity of the family.' Through returning to this most primitive of all human relationships, artificial dams and barriers are swept away and the possibility of a *free flow* restored.

In regard to the Reclining Figure motif, the symbolism is less obvious. Read suggests the influence of the Mexican reclining god on whose flattened torso sacrifices were offered: again we see the body as sometimes excavated, sometimes split asunder, sometimes straining towards the upright in which it begins to approximate to another sacrificial motif, the Cross or Crucifixion. Somehow, it seems, we are in the presence of an archetypal image of travail, of life bursting the bands of death, of the triumph of sacrifice.[4] Whether this is the most significant image that will finally stand out from Moore's work I am in no position to say. But few men have exercised so universal an appeal simply through variations on the two great themes which have obsessed him.

[4] Cp. Moore's own words: 'No one really knows anything unless he knows also the opposite. I personally believe that all life is a conflict: that's something to be accepted, something you have to know. And you have to die, too, which is the opposite of living. One must try to find a synthesis to come to terms with opposite qualities. Art and life are made up of conflicts.'

In his essay on Matisse, Read shows how great was this artist's indebtedness to Cézanne but he does not deal with the latter's work in detail. Yet it could be claimed that Cézanne is an outstanding example of a painter who exposed himself without reserve to the seemingly uncontrollable flux of things and at the same time achieved through his art marvels of reconciliation and endurance. For him nature was no settled order of things whose formal structures could be immediately discerned and represented in art. Instead he was to speak of 'the torrent of the world'. 'All that we see,' he said to Gasquet, 'is dispersed, is transient, is it not? Nature is always the same but nothing remains of what we see of her endurance, with the ingredients, the appearance of all her changes'.

Clearly Cézanne was reacting strongly against a long-established tradition of painting in which the composition of ideal forms, the recognition of approved subjects, the reflection of recurring shapes, took pride of place. He for his part was determined to be free, to open out, as it were, a free flow between his own sensations and the totality of the natural world which formed the field of his vision. So he was able to give the sense of enormous vitality: even the apples and oranges in what is designated 'Still Life' are on the point it seems of bursting out into movement and change. The picture as a whole gives the sense of what I have called 'free flow' among its colours and contours and varying elements and this corresponds to the free flow of sensation for which Cézanne had striven almost with desperation. At all costs he must respond through his own sensations to a world in movement, dynamic, free.

Yet the wonderful correlative of the sense of flux in his pictures was the equally strong sense of depth and endurance and repose. The 'integrating image' may not be immediately obvious but it is never absent. Somehow the elements which are alive and straining towards the movement are held together and in a very real sense *reconciled* with one another. In *The Mont Sainte-Victoire seen from Bellevue* the firm horizontal of the road and the strong vertical of the house provide an ordered framework through which the whole picture gains a satisfying integration.

In a remarkable broadcast entitled 'Polarity', David Sylvester summarized the particular contribution of Cézanne in this way:

'In our lives nothing troubles us more than our inability to deal with those contradictions which we recognize in ourselves, in our feelings, our desires, our consciences—our inability to accept them and reconcile them. We tend to deal with such contradictions by closing our minds to the existence of one side or another or by evading them with some feeble compromise. Perhaps it is because Cézanne's art accepts contradictions to the full and finds a means to reconcile them that we always feel instinctively that it means so infinitely more than its ostensible subject. What it means is a moral grandeur which we cannot find in ourselves.

'Among the contradictions which his art presents there is none, perhaps, more profound than that between the sense of the transience of life and of its permanence. In the 'Still Life with Teapot', even more, even much more, in the great late paintings of Mont Sainte-Victoire, we experience these contradictory feelings separately, and each as poignantly as the other. There is a hopeless sadness that all we see and rejoice in dies for us no sooner than it is seen; there is a serene affirmation that what we are now looking at will be there for ever. We are faced with our deepest concerns about life and our place in it, but exalted here by this total acceptance of the intolerable fact that mortality and immortality are only meaningful in relation to each other.'

As I have suggested, Cézanne first gave the imagination a new freedom, a freedom to respond sensitively to the world's constant flux. But it was not to be an uncontrolled freedom. Rather by means of an integrating framework, if not an integrating image, contradictions were reconciled and order affirmed.

In addition to sculpture and painting, and probably exercising an even more powerful influence, there is the art of music. Already certain controlled experiments have been carried out in mental hospitals to estimate the effects upon patients of the transmission of certain types of music. It has been found for example that romantic music often produces emotional release but does not tend towards group cohesion. On the other hand classical music appears to give more security, presumably because of its more formal structure. Yet the most striking result of all is that traditional and folk songs have proved themselves to be the most powerful agents in increasing the harmony and integration of any particular group. This music, based on it is on deep-seated human and cosmic relationships, binds people together whether they are normal or emotionally disturbed.[5]

What emerges in a general and suggestive way from such enquiries is reinforced when reference is made to a particular and outstanding modern composer. Benjamin Britten has been constantly concerned with the convergence of opposites. And as he has expressed this concern musically he has constantly had recourse to the themes of innocence and sacrifice. Innocence we naturally associate with childhood, with the free and uninhibited flow of emotions and gestures and language. Britten has excelled in composing music such as 'A Ceremony of Carols' and 'Noye's Fludde' in which discordant elements are brought together and sung out in joyful abandon. The sweet and the sentimental have no place for they have no place in the typical emotions of childhood. The essential mark of the child is a wondering innocence (as in Billy Budd), an innocence which must in some measure be restored to us if we are to find the resolution of the strains and tensions which so soon characterize our lives. And music can relieve the tension and release new energies as it grasps the dissonances and integrates them into song.

At a deeper level, however, there needs to be an image which can hold together the ultimate contradictions of human experience —death and life, violence and serenity, filth and purity, implacability and forgiveness. It has ever been the distinction of the greatest artists to reconcile these opposites rather than to adopt some weak compromise or some partisan emphasis. And in the case of Britten the theme which has captivated his own attention and which he is obviously deeply concerned to express through his music is the theme of sacrifice. Supremely in his work so far the opposites are reconciled in the *War Requiem*. Through the juxtaposition of Wilfred Owen's bitter poems arising out of the 1914–18 War with Latin sections of the traditional Requiem, Britten draws together life's ghastly contradictories within the sacrifice of the Lamb of God; only as man cries out:

O Lamb of God that takest away the sins
    of the world, have mercy upon us,

can he begin to tread the pathway which leads towards true peace.

The combination of the two themes of innocence and sacrifice

---

[5] See Sydney D. Mitchell, *Music in Mental Hospitals*; quoted in H. Lowery, *The Background of Music* (Hutchinson, 1952), 186.

was strikingly pointed up by the Music Critic of the *Times* on the occasion of the celebration of Britten's fiftieth birthday:

'The innocent,' he wrote, 'may be a happy, dirty, driving boy, or a brother and sister possessed by ghosts, or the rustic buffoon who strayed into fairyland, or the swearing soldier in the trenches. In him, we are made to feel, is a blessedness that was once common to us all, but that most of us have lost. The sacrifice may be no more than an artistic limitation, like Wordsworth's sonnet: or it may be a permanent deprivation with a positively beneficial effect, a metamorphosis; or it may be a ritual murder. These two essentially religious themes are central to his art, and they are the more impressive because he presents them always with a certain abstraction, a preference for understatement. Even in the most powerful, apparently loaded of all his compositions, the personal indictment of war is scrupulously set against the more massive, impersonal consolation of ecclesiastical liturgy, as if to ensure that we who listen must ourselves take the responsibility for our final impression.'

Finally I propose to make brief reference to the literary arts in which—whether in poetry or drama or the novel—the theme of alienation constantly appears and in which, less frequently but when it happens even more powerfully, a way of reconciliation is defined. What Coleridge wrote about the work of the poet seems to me equally applicable to the novelist and dramatist. This representative individual 'brings the whole soul of man into activity. He diffuses a tone and a spirit that blends and as it were fuses (the faculties) each into each by that synthetic and magical power to which I would exclusively appropriate the name of imagination. This power reveals itself in the balance or reconcilement of discordant qualities— a more than usual state of emotion with more than usual order'.

This 'reconcilement' I suggest is primarily effected by the juxtaposition of images in such a way as *either* to bring about release, the restoration of free flow, the openness to change *or* to bring together in an integrated form, to establish a momentary reconciliation, to point the way to the ultimate union. And the first of these operations is most easily achieved by bringing together aspects of present experience with those of an earlier age —of childhood (whether of the individual or of the race), of innocence, of Eden (Edwin Muir's 'One Foot in Eden'). Whether it be Wordsworth turning back in memory to his childhood emotions of desire and fear, whether it be William Golding turning back in *Free Fall* to a boy's struggles, the result is the same. The very juxtaposition of what seems to be an adult straight-jacket of habit and routine with the openness and flux and variations of childhood and above all of days of innocence, seems to initiate a process of unlocking doors, of re-opening questions which seemed to be closed, of restoring movement and hope.

Yet by itself this is not enough. There needs also to be the integrating image, the potential meeting-point, the structure which can bring together the still discordant elements which have gained release. And this image gains form and expression, it would seem, supremely through the juxtaposition of the contraries of experience which belong to every age—sacrifice and tragedy and vicarious suffering and heroic self-abandonment. Whether it be the Suffering Servant or the evangel of the crucified Christ the resultant combination of 'more than usual emotion', with 'more than usual order' is basically the same. The very juxtaposition of images and experiences which defy any purely logical connection can in an ultimately inexplicable way bring peace and calm to the human spirit.

For me a favourite example of the intertwining of the two motifs is to be found in T. S. Eliot's 'Four Quartets'. On the one hand there are the imaginative returns to ancestral and childhood experiences. East Coker, the village in Somerset from which in the 17th century his ancestors set out for the New World, the brown river Mississippi near which he was born, the rocky New England coast, where he played as a boy—these 'Edens' are recalled, the rhythm of the nursery bedroom, the voices of the sea, the inno-cence of country mirth. Above all there is the vivid image of

the children in the apple-tree
Not known, because not looked for
But heard, half-heard, in the stillness
Between two waves of the sea.

The poet himself is at middle age, a turning point of uncertainty. It is by confronting his own present state with the early images of innocence and laughter and hope, that the process of release and redemption begins and the prospect of some fuller reconciliation comes into sight.

But besides the images of innocence there are the awe-inspiring images of sacrifice. None is more impressive than the Poem on the Passion which forms the fourth movement of the Second of the Quartets. In this the juxtaposition of contraries seems to reach extreme limits. In the hospital, the building which Philip Rieff has called the archetypal institution of western culture, life faces death, the healing art grapples with sickness, the hard steel probes the exquisitely sensitive wound, the way to restoration is by growing worse, the heat of fever coincides with the body's freezing chill:

> The dripping blood our only drink,
> The bloody flesh our only food:
> In spite of which we like to think
> That we are sound, substantial flesh and blood—
> Again, in spite of that, we call this Friday good.

Nowhere that I know in modern literature are the opposites, the contraries, the antagonisms of living experience expressed more starkly, more relentlessly. Yet nowhere is there evidence of a profounder faith that in this very bringing together of the opposites, without compromise or dissimulation, the artist creates a word-structure corresponding to the ultimate reality of reconciliation and peace. Mr. Eliot does not compel our assent, he does not opt for any easy reconciliation. But that even here on earth it was possible to experience intimations of the ultimate reconciliation, of this, his own profound conviction, the poet leaves us in no doubt. He expresses it beautifully as early as the second movement of the first of the Quartets, Burnt Norton:

> Garlic and sapphires in the mud
> Clot the bedded axle-tree.
> The trilling wire in the blood
> Sings below inveterate scars
> Appeasing long-forgotten wars.
> The dance along the artery
> The circulation of the lymph
> Are figured in the drift of stars
> Ascend to summer in the tree
> We move above the moving tree
> In light upon the figured leaf
> And hear upon the sodden floor

> Below, the boarhound and the boar
> Pursue their pattern as before
> But reconciled among the stars.

On the sodden floor alienation may seem the obvious descriptive word: it is the poet who sees beyond to the 'reconcilement' among the stars.

VI

PURPOSE AND CHOICE

B. Babington Smith

i

The terms Purpose and Choice carry overtones of philosophical arguments about predestination, free will and the impossibility of finding room in a chain of cause and effect for the intervention of voluntary acts.

On whether man is free, Kant (I find in translation) held that 'every being who can act only under the idea that he is free is, for that very reason, also in practice free, i.e. all the laws that are inseparably connected with freedom hold for him *as if* his will had been declared free, both in itself and by the criteria of theoretical philosophy. I therefore claim that every rational individual who possesses a will, must necessarily also be endowed with the idea of freedom according to which alone he acts'. An explanatory remark follows:

'Thus the same laws hold good for a being who can act only under the idea of his own freedom, that would bind one who really was free.'

This view, quoted in his *Philosophy of As If*, Vaihinger assimilated with his own; but William James in *Varieties of Religious Experience* called it a particularly uncouth part of Kant's philosophy.

Much philosophical writing is concerned less with what *is* the case than with what views are coherent with one another and follow logically from their premises. In this strain Professor Broad (*Mind and its Place in Nature*, p. 490) considers Kant's argument and concludes, with suitable reservations, that it proves its conclusions; but on the next page doubts whether 'Kant's ethical argument proves that we are 'free' in any sense of 'freedom' which could not have been established by direct inspection, and all these senses seem to me to be probably consistent with complete determinism'.

Professor Hart in his recent book[1] treats of implications of free will and determinism in bringing Punishment and Responsibility under the philosophical magnifying glass.

Writers of such critical works may remain uncommitted to any of the views they discuss. When asked if he believed some view to which he had just given expression, one of the best known answered, 'Well I wouldn't go to the stake for it, if indeed I would go to the stake for anything'.

But I am not here concerned with whether man *is* or *is not* free, nor indeed am I concerned whether a man is always rational and consistent with himself. It is not given to all of us to be like a certain other well-known philosopher, who, as the anecdote had it, being persuaded by argument that he had no reasonable grounds for gloom, cheered up.

I am concerned rather with ordinary men's outlooks, ideas, behaviour and what they exemplify.

One can find statements illustrating extreme positions. At the one, in the words of Omar Khayyam, not unassisted by Fitzgerald:

> What, out of senseless nothing to provoke
> A conscious something to resist the yoke
>   Of unpermitted pleasure under pain
>   Of everlasting penalties if broke.
>
> O thou, who didst with pitfall and with gin
> Beset the road I was to wander in,
>   Thou wilt not with predestined evil round
>   Enmesh and then impute my fall to sin.

And somewhere near the other extreme I find the following paragraph: 'Fellow Christians and fellow citizens, should such things continue? I would say no, and thus I plead for a home to which any body may be sent, his case inquired into and a helping hand extended to him, until he can labour for himself.

It is only by such means that crime can be lessened in our juvenile population, for criminals are of the worst class who are so from their youth, and cost a thousand times more for the cure than for the prevention of crime: in fact I believe it can't be cured, but I am sure it might be prevented.'

This is an extract from the letter written by William Quarrier

[1] *Punishment and Responsibility*, (Oxford, 1968).

to the Press in 1871, which led to the foundation of the Orphan Homes of Scotland. (William Quarrier, p. 77: Alexander Gammie). In similar vein are the following words:

'Laws wisely administered will secure men in the enjoyment of the fruits of their labour, whether of mind or body, at a comparatively small personal sacrifice; but no laws however stringent will make the idle industrious, the thriftless provident, or the drunken sober. Such reforms can only be effected by means of individual action, economy and self-denial; by better habits, rather than by greater rights'.

This was written by Samuel Smiles in *Self Help* (p. 2).

But it does not take great thinkers or writers to think in deterministic terms, to see effects following causes or to follow purposes.

Wise sayings and proverbs could be quoted in plenty. 'Eat, drink and be merry. . . ." "Take no heed for the morrow. . . ." "Look before you leap" . . . 'Heaven helps those who help themselves' are but instances, and almost always advice pointing in one direction can be matched by advice pointing the other way. As if caught in some isometric exercise where muscle opposes muscle the cumulative wisdom of mankind seems to bar the way to itself. Walking, by contrast, takes one forward and in what follows I shall try to show a way.

ii

Once upon a time there were three men in a railway carriage. The first sat with his back to the engine watching the trees and fields receding into the distance and thinking about the course of events which had brought him where he was. The second, facing the engine, saw the landscape grow and flash by while he considered the object of his journey and what he was going to do.

This third man said 'This is a very comfortable compartment; it is very gratifying to travel first class'.

The three men in the story are Freud, Jung and Adler. While the story could be expanded to bring in allusions to all sorts of features of their teaching what I have told is enough to make my point.

Outlook in time offers a crucial basis of comparison between these three great psychotherapists.

Freud, travelling with his back to the engine looks to the past. The future is out of sight behind him. Using the 'figure-ground' concept, the past is the *figure* for him; the future and all concerned with it is in the *ground*. Now instincts are forward-looking, so for Freud they and their influence are not in the figure, but in the ground. The term which Freud used for this situation of being 'out of sight' or 'in the ground' is 'unconscious'. Freud was explicitly concerned to find out how a patient had come to his present state, and it was explicitly (at any rate at one stage) his doctrine that the acceptance by the patient of the origins of his condition, as they were recovered by the process of psychoanalysis, constituted the cure.

Jung travelling with his face to the engine looks to what is ahead; the past is behind him. So for Jung purpose is explicit, it is in the figure, and it is conscious; but the past history stretches behind out of sight and, using the figure-ground principle again, is in the unconscious. If we think of ways in which we now function as having developed through the past history of the race, i.e., that we inherit not only our physical body but also its functioning, and the ways in which it can function because of its construction, then these will, for the Jungian, be 'in the ground' and 'out of the figure', that is, out of consciousness. These ways of functioning give the 'archetypes' which influence our thinking and in terms of which we think, and are to a great extent shared with our fellows.

Adler was concerned with adaptation to present circumstance, and realization of the life style of the person, as a means to power.

Thus the contrast I want to draw at the conscious level is between Freud's concern with cause and explanation, Jung's with purpose and meaning, Adler's with power and adaptation.

Let me support these views with quotations. Lewis Way (*Adler's Place in Psychology*) in comparing Freud and Adler says, 'One can picture psychoanalysis as Freud himself pictured the dream. As a regressive movement away from the external world down the long corridor that leads to childhood, narcissistic individualism, the mother's comforting womb until it ends in the final death wish. Its philosophy is that of an austere pessimism'.

When Freud's theories hit Europe in the early years of this century it was not so much the sexuality which caused dismay as the complete determinism involved.

Quoting again from Lewis Way, 'The analytical technique initiated by Freud is a far more formidable instrument than

Socrates ever possessed. Adler makes use of it, not so much to unravel the causal mechanisms of the symptom as to build a complete picture of the patient's life style. . . . The charge of partiality seems to be the most serious charge that can be laid against Adler, and should I think be constantly borne in mind. It consists in seeing life too much from the extraverted view point of *Adaptation to the external conditions of the environment* (my italics). The problems of life are not, of course, as simple as mere adaptation, and, while it would be unfair to Adler to suppose that he imagined that they were, his insistence on this aspect of life may have laid him open to misinterpretation.'

Jung in his preface to the second edition of *Collected Papers on Analytical Psychology* had this to say: 'Dr. Mitchell in his review takes exception to my heresy respecting causality. He considers I am entering a perilous, because unscientific course when I question the sole validity of the causal view point in psychology. I sympathise with him, but in my opinion the nature of the human mind compels us to take the final point of view. For it cannot be disputed that psychologically speaking we are living and working, day by day, according to the principle of directed aim or purpose, as well as that of causality. . . .

'We must always bear the fact in mind that *causality is a point of view*. . . . *Finality is also a view point*, that is justified empirically solely by the existence of a series of events wherein the causal connection is indeed evident, but *the meaning of which only becomes intelligible as producing a final effect*' (my italics).

To summarize, I propose, as a useful over-simplification, that Freud was concerned to trace the origin of trouble and believed that realization and acceptance constituted the cure: 'The more fully the causal reason underlying a state is revealed the more fully is it explained.' To a non-Freudian it seems that patients may feel enormously relieved by Freudian treatment, but they do not know what to do next, and the old sequence is likely to happen again. Jung was concerned with purpose and meaning, but, to the extent that Jung is dealing with the future, his answers cannot be given in terms of fact; and anyone involved in this system must come to terms with the use of symbols and principles.

Adler was concerned with inferiority complexes, with compensation for defects, and the will to power. These are all valuable concepts, but what was the power for? He has no answer, any more than to the question, what is adaptation for?

Proponents of each of the three schools of thought were concerned to argue that they were right and that the others were wrong.

Glover for example is explicit on the point and will consider no compromise. 'If Freud is right, Jung is nothing more or less than an academic (conscious) psychologist masquerading as the apostle of a new dynamic psychology. If Jung is right, Freud's system should be dismissed as the symptomatic expression of a psycho-pathological character, valid only for those who suffer from similar obsessions.'

But once one has seen the relevance of the time relationships involved, the question of the rightness or wrongness of the three positions shrinks in importance. It becomes comparable to the question as to which is the right way to see a reversible figure.

Among ordinary men you can find examples of the same three outlooks, as my quotations may have illustrated, and a view-point which makes good sense to one man may seem wilful perversion of experience to another. If such men can come to see the extent to which their differences arise from outlooks, understanding may be achieved, or even agreement.

In a discussion of the saying 'There are no bad pupils, only bad teachers', I heard a scientifically trained man assert firmly that the truth of this statement simply depended upon the facts, and what were the facts? The view which prevailed and which he finally accepted, was that, whatever the facts, this would be a good motto for any teacher to hang upon his wall and that its comple-ment 'There are no bad teachers, only bad pupils' might well be on every pupil's desk. In demanding the facts he was looking back to the past, while the acceptance of the saying as a guide is to face forward.

Matters might be simple if everyone belonged to one or other of three classes and either faced forward or backward or lived in the present. But they are not so simple, nor do men always behave in the same way; nor is it part of my case that they do or should. In fact, it is of the greatest importance to a man to be able to plan for the future and to analyse the past, and his life will be the poorer if he cannot at times lay aside care and criticism and enjoy himself here and now.

The same triple division of outlook can be seen in the scientific field. Karl Pearson envisaged science claiming the whole field of knowledge for her domain and her function as that of describing not explaining (*Grammar of Science*, 1892, p. 335).

'The growth of knowledge since the days of Aristotle ought to be sufficient to convince us that we have no reason to despair of man's ultimate mastering any problem whatever of life or mind, however obscure and difficult it may at present appear. But we ought to remember what this mastery means; it does not denote an explanation of the routine of perception: it is solely the description of that routine in brief conceptual formulae. It is the historical resumé, not the transcendental exegesis of final causes'.

There spoke another man with his back to the engine.

Grensted (*Psychology and God*, 1928, p. 21) wrote, 'The whole method and aim of experimental psychology is to reduce to a minimum those aspects of human behaviour which are indeterminate and impredictable', and six lines later, 'The fundamental presupposition of all this is determinism, the operation of the strict laws of cause and effect'.

Thus Grensted placed the experimental psychologists of the day in the same group, with their backs to the engine too. For such people 'why?' means 'in what way?' or 'what was the cause?'

A different emphasis comes into the writings of scientists with the new discoveries in physics and new theories of cosmology. Martin Johnson (*Time, Knowledge and Nebulae*, 1945, p. 47): 'A misleading development was that causality, when elevated to a Principle supposed necessary to scientific inference, became a criterion of absolute time sequence: if all events are causes or effects, for any pair the label of "cause" was held to mark conclusively the antecedent in time.' A few lines later he wrote, "It therefore seems that "Functional dependences giving communicability of laws" might be a more reliable description that is sought in physical investigations than "sequences of cause and effect".' Here the aim of the scientist has changed and his concern is with concomitant variation or statistical correlation between variables. The question is no longer 'what was the cause of what?' but 'what varies with what?' Note that time need not be in the picture, and compare this view with Lewin's theory that everything relevant to one's next state is present now; that there is no question of the influence of memories from the past or of fears of the future, they cannot be relevant unless they operate here and now. In such a situation the question why? is like that variety of the child's 'why?' described by Susan Isaacs as 'an undifferentiated request for more information' (*Intellectual Growth of Young Children*, p. 327).

Dingle (*Through Science to Philosophy*, 1937, p. 275) gives reasons for the tenacity with which we cling to universal causality. Then later he turns to the joint effect of the quantum theory and statistical mechanics and writes (p. 289): 'The net result of these discoveries is that science no longer seeks for certainty, but only for the probability that an event will occur or that a natural law is true—or, in short, that anything is anything. This means that all its statements are of a statistical character.' And later (p. 315): 'Can we say that will is free? If freedom means absence of relations with other constituents of the psychological molecule then its freedom is a measure of the incompleteness of psychology. An unrelated will is not a scientific concept, it is a superstition. We use will to co-ordinate actions; 'in the circumstances I decided to do so and so', this means that the circumstances and the act are rationally connected by the will, and to say that one's will is not free is merely to say one acts rationally and not capriciously.'

Recently concern with abuse and misapplication of discoveries and new techniques has led some scientists to ask the question 'why?' meaning 'what for?' I believe it would be a grave mistake to suppose that man should ask this question on the grounds that it is properly something only a scientist should ask. This is something that men as men should be concerned with.

Scientists however have difficulty with this outlook. Lorenz for instance (*Aggression*, p. 72): 'What is an instinct? The terms often used for various instinctual motivations are frequently tainted by the unfortunate heritage of 'finalistic' thinking. A 'finalist' in this bad sense of the word is someone who confuses the question 'what for?' with the question 'why?' and thus believes that by demonstrating the species-preserving reason for a certain function he has solved the problem of its causation'.

Miller Galanter and Pribram in *Plans and the Structure of Behaviour* (p. 59) in the chapter called 'Values, Intention and the execution of plans', quote, C. I. Lewis's references to Intent, saying, 'The term "intent" is Lewis's way of trying to catch this elusive and unique feature of the behaviour of living systems.

'In speaking in these terms he is like any ordinary person who tries to say what makes his actions meaningful—but he is quite unlike most experimental psychologists. Intention went out of style as a psychological concept when reflex theory and its derivatives became the foundation of our scientific theories of behaviour. . . . And most of the explicit uses that have occurred (in the past twenty years) can probably be traced to the influence of Kurt Lewin'. A little further on they write (p. 161), 'For Lewin there is a complete parallel between the dynamics of intention and the dynamics of any other motivated behaviour. It is this dynamic property of an intention that we feel is confusing and we wish to reformulate it'. It is very clear if one reads Lewin's treatment of intention that, the more he says, the more clearly intention becomes something *representable in the present* by a 'Valence'.

The three attitudes exhibited in these views about science are drawn from a period extending over some 80 years and I think it is indicative of the way outlook has changed that they move from concern with cause and effect to concern with concomitant variation and that in recent years there have been increasing signs of concern with purpose.

iii

In every-day life one finds all three outlooks and it is of interest to consider how they affect several 'regions of discourse'. I select four; the first may be broadly designated morality, the second road traffic control, the third views on intelligence and the fourth planning.

Related to morality is a wide range of concepts, of which praise, blame, reward, punishment, guilt, responsibility, merit, will, character, and conscience should suffice to illustrate my point.

If we face the future, all these terms have intelligible and well established meanings and have coherent relationships when used of a being who has purposes and can choose. Praise and reward or blame and punishment concern the encouraging or discouraging of activities. They can be used to raise standards or prevent shortcomings. Each must be tempered to the case, for any one of them carried to excess can be destructive.

Guilt[2] in this setting has its real value as a state of distress,

---

[2] A theologian would here say 'sense of guilt' instead of 'guilt'. (Ed.)

arising from a consciousness of shortcoming or transgression, which may be expunged by forgiveness or worked off by restitution. Responsibility has two faces, a man's feeling of responsibility stemming from an acknowledgement of, and acceptance of, obligations; while the other, for which perhaps accountability could be a more useful term, arises where others see him as being under obligations. Rudolf Allers, writing avowedly as a Roman Catholic, stressed the value of punishment in the formation of character (*The Psychology of Character*, pp. 102–119).

If, however, we look to the past and think in terms of cause and effect the pattern of morality falls to pieces. In a determinist system, responsibility, choice, merit and demerit are inapplicable concepts (as Professor Ryle says in *The Concept of Mind*, London, 1949, p. 20). They are no longer applicable in the sense outlined above in relation to a forward-looking standpoint. But that does not prevent one who 'travels with his back to the engine' from using the terms. For instance, Professor Hart in his chapter on 'Legal Responsibility and Excuses' in *Punishment and Responsibility*, Oxford, 1968, states two claims that a determinist would have to make and ends that for such a man, 'Consequently to allow punishment to depend on the presence or absence of excusing conditions, or to think it justified when they are absent but not when they are present is absurd, meaningless, irrational, unjust or immoral or perhaps all of these.'
and in a footnote:

'Of course if we knew the laws and could use them for the detailed and exact prediction of our own and others' conduct *deliberation* and *choice* would become pointless, and perhaps in such circumstances these could not (logically) be 'deliberation' or 'choice' (op. cit., p. 29).

Freudians talk about guilt, but in a Freudian system guilt becomes irrational. It is an unreasonable burden and the treatment has been to relieve a man of guilt by leading him to understand that it is a meaningless psychological burden in such a setting. A man needs to learn to express himself, to realize himself, and, if he assimilates the system, comes to do so without the inconvenience of guilt. Morals lose authority; though customs and morals are liable to develop in any society. Praise and blame become names for pleasant or unpleasant consequences; so do reward and punishment; none then have constructive functions, since they arise as reactions to action. They may restore a balance that has been disturbed, as in the principle of an eye for an eye and a tooth for a tooth.

In his letters Freud wrote that he expected to find the physical cause lying behind morality and in a letter 5 Nov. 1897 gave his explanation of 'morality shame, etc.'.

If, as a third possibility, we consider these terms without looking forward or back, we may observe interesting correlations. We can talk of the frequency with which men accused of crimes are caught and receive sentences; the evenness of the distribution of honours, or the risks of making mistakes. There is no value in praise or blame here, other than pleasantness or unpleasantness. It is unpleasant to be caught; the only thing is not to be caught. The tone is statistical and one deals in risks and probabilities. A guess or choice may be correct or incorrect, risky or damaging, but neither right nor wrong, neither good nor bad. As information accrues one may know better which horse to back, which stock to buy, what gives offence or ensures popularity. Here again the terms responsibility or guilt can be used, but their meanings have changed, they carry no moral overtones and whole tenor of life has changed.

In any social situation we may find men adopting different standpoints and then there are liable to be misunderstandings. For instance in a court of law, a judge may adopt a purposive outlook while the accused takes a determinist standpoint, that he had no option. At the same time an onlooker may see this as but another instance contributing to the statistics of delinquency and sentence after conviction. I do not even wish to suppose that any one man always adopts the same outlook. I must also make it clear that I do not wish to suggest that everyone who faces forwards is a Jungian or backwards a Freudian. These two well-known systems allow me to illustrate how an interchange of figure and ground can be used to relate two apparently incompatible views of life.

Turning to my next example, the number of people driving on the roads increases steadily. The performance of road vehicles rises steadily too. The number of accidents and deaths is a very high price for the convenience of road transport. Approaching this situation from the aspect of cause and effect, one may say, for instance, this corner is dangerous so either it must be altered to

H

be less dangerous, or drivers must be warned of the danger by a sign. Cross roads are dangerous, so either must they be altered or motorists warned, or motorists must be controlled by traffic lights so that only one stream of traffic can cross at one time. Speed contributes to accidents so speed must be controlled. In each case a source of danger is lessened by the motorist obeying a sign or signal. The more this is done, the more driving is reduced to obeying signals; the more this is so, the more signals drivers will need.

If, however, we look forward, the purpose of a driving test is to ensure that the driver has a sufficient measure of control of his car to drive safely on the road. If he has not a sufficient measure of control, what he needs is more training and more experience. When the driver has gained more experience, and has learnt to drive better, he will be less likely to be involved in an accident. Thus, there are two distinct ways of approaching road safety. One is based on looking back to the causes of accidents, and involves increasing the number of signs controlling roads so that drivers have no judgements to make; they have only to obey signals. The other, looking forward and developing purpose, is designed to ensure that judgement and driving skill are increased, in which case control signals will become progressively less necessary.

In practice, a combination of both road signals and further training may produce even better results. But this would not affect the point that one approach is indicated by emphasis on cause and effect and the other by a purposive outlook.

My third instance comes from the educational field. Mental tests were developed in the early 1900's, and by the 20's the so-called Intelligence Quotient was in fairly common use. There was a theory current that intelligence tests could reveal the *native* intelligence of one who was tested and since this would not change the intelligence quotient should remain constant. One of the real achievements of the mental test was to identify children whose I.Q. set them much higher in relation to their fellows than did achievement tests, such as of English or arithmetic, as a result of which their real capacity was recognized and developed. In 1924 the Board of Education's Committee 'The Hadow Committee',[3]

---

[3] *Psychological Tests of Educable Capacity and their Possible Use in the Public System of Education* is its full title.

in its report accepted the theory that tests could reveal native intelligence. The claim was of very great importance for educational practice; since, if a child's native level was known, his performance in school could be assessed as being above or below expectation and the course and final level of his development could be forecast.

The claim, if warranted, constitutes a firm theoretical basis for selection at any age, and, since the admirable reservations made by the Hadow Committee were forgotten, the practical implications of its being widely accepted can be seen in the development of the 11 plus examination with its reliance on I.Q. tests.

Subsequent experience led many to suspect that the situation was not so straightforward and that children's showing, even on the most orthodox Intelligence tests, could be improved by coaching. Professor Vernon in an important piece of research produced evidence of considerable increases in I.Q.s after coaching, and the evidence, as summarised by him (*British Journal of Educational Psychology*, 1954 Symposium, Pt. V) was enough to shake the faith even of those who constructed 'I.Q. tests'. I take it as a sign of this that the name of the Moray House Tests were changed at about this time from Intelligence tests to tests of Verbal Reasoning.

There were still those who said 'nothing has changed; these tests are the same except for the name'. But the change was of the utmost significance, since it undermined the claim to measure native intelligence. Professor Vernon's finding destroyed more than he ever claimed, for the effects of coaching are two-fold. Not only may scores on a test or type of test be raised to some extent but, what is more important, coaching affects the *meaning* of the score. To take a very simple example from arithmetic, if a child is asked what is 16 by 13, three main situations can arise. First that the child does not know what multiplication is, and then the question is outside his scope; secondly, he may have learnt some of his tables, so that the form of the question is familiar and also a means for working it out is available to him; thirdly, if the child has learnt what 16 by 13 is, he knows the answer.

Coaching takes a pupil away from one end of the scale towards the other. In the first state, if the correct answer is given it can only be a guess, in the third case it is a matter of memory, while intermediately, when the question is on the fringe of the child's knowledge, intelligence will be involved in answering. Out of this approach comes the principle that no question need, of its nature, be a test of intelligence; but any question, given the appropriate circumstances, may be.

The net effect of these developments is that faith in the idea that native intelligence can be revealed by tests is severely shaken. The I.Q. can only be regarded as the measure obtained at a certain time, for a certain child, by a certain test under certain conditions. It remains open then that I.Q. may rise or fall in the future. The question now becomes not to select children who have native intelligence at certain levels or of certain kinds for certain kinds of education, but rather, now that the child is freed to a great extent from his past history, to lay plans for the most effective educational course for him for the future.

Thus with the retreat from a theory of a fixed innate intelligence determining the possibilities for the future, the new position allows and encourages a forward-looking approach and planning for the most productive future (a view which must be kept distinct from the view that there should be no streaming). In this instance a theory about cause and effect can be seen affecting the whole system of selection and planning in education.

It is not only in education that the outlook affects planning. If one faces the past and thinks in terms of cause and effect planning becomes a matter of considering the possible courses of action. Thus a determinist planner must produce the possible sequences of events flowing from the present state. He may assess the value of desirability of the various possible outcomes, and it will be for someone to choose which to try to follow (whatever such choice can mean to a determinist).

Another way of planning, one which I should like to associate with a forward facung outlook, may be derived by expanding ideas put forward earlier. If one "faces the engine" one cannot deal in terms of facts or events, but must accustom oneself to using symbols, and principles and generalisations. On this basis planning takes on a distinctive character. Facing forwards one can state the principles or standards which will guide one's actions towards an objective. The resulting planning will be more like navigating by compass or stars than like following an A.A. route.

If these two types of planning, both of which may be encountered in ordinary life, are typical of travelling with one's back to the engine or facing it respectively, what about the man whose concern is in the present? I suggest that for such people planning is uncongenial and unfamiliar, and that it is among such that are those who, when things go well, live for the present, but are liable to be overwhelmed in the expedients of 'crisis management' when things go wrong. By 'crisis management' I mean a state in which action is reaction to sudden and unexpected change. When there is no planning, all changes come as sudden and as unexpected. There are other ways; some may be useful. But I find the statement by Miller Galanter and Pribram that 'so long as people are behaving some plan or other must be executed' is one I cannot even acquiesce in.

In practice, of course, it may be advisable to have at one's disposal all three outlooks referred to above so that they may supplement each other. But I have observed that a man who has developed one of the three methods described may not be aware of other possibilities and may seek to persuade others to follow his example. In short, some individuals tend to face forwards and think, live and act in terms of purpose, or to face backwards and see life as an inevitable succession of effects of causes, or to think in terms of the present and of observable concomitant variation.

iv

I have tried to show what a difference it makes to one's outlook to face one way or the other and to the meanings which one will attach to some very important terms. This theme can be extended from the effects on individuals to the effects on groups. Here I draw on experience of work with groups of managers, mostly from what is called 'middle management'. For these opportunities I wish to acknowledge my great indebtedness to Mr. R. Coverdale. Group is a very general term; here I am concerned with groups of human beings. In the society of today we find an almost infinite variety of groups. If we use the term to mean two or more people who have some attribute in common for a period of time, we shall include all and many more than all the groups I have in mind, but it may make it easier to see that most of us are at one time or another members of groups. For instance, one man asking another the way gives, for that time, a group of two. People in a bus queue are a group; so are the people in a railway compartment. A married couple is a special sort of group, and so is a football team.

So in a different way is the same football team together with its trainer, Club managers and supporters.

It is a characteristic of many groups that the members regard themselves as having interests in common, that they distinguish members from non-members, as when a seventh enters a railway compartment when six seats are occupied. Many groups may be regarded as active in that the members embark on projects. One of the surprising things about such groups is how difficult it is to achieve what might seem essential, namely, agreement about projects to be undertaken.

If men in a group begin to argue about some project, it is always possible to ask 'why should it be undertaken?' If the answer to this is accepted by all, then there is a common basis for progress. If, however, the answer given to this question still provokes argument, one can ask 'why' again. When this is repeatedly done, the answer tends to become more general; but one would not have embarked on an infinite regress, because in practice one could reach a level of generality at which all could agree, and from this level one could go forward.

A procedure devised by Mr. Coverdale for studying this situation was for each man in a group to write his answers independently, and to continue asking and answering why alternately till he could go no further. Using this procedure the answers of a number of groups to successive questions why? were obtained and considered. One of the first findings was that some people habitually understand 'why' as 'for what purpose', facing the future, while others, just as spontaneously it seems, take it in the sense 'for what reason' and face the past. An answer typical of the former is 'in order to improve my salary' and of the latter 'because my boss sent me'.

Some more generalizations about such answers can be offered. Men differ widely in their time scales: some in this situation give evidence of thinking much further into the future than others. As the questions go deeper different interests emerge: home, business prospects, national politics or the welfare of mankind. Perhaps, if the matter were fully explored, all of them would turn out to be in the picture, though the relative importance attached to home or business or country would vary from one man to another. Some will offer a basis on which two men or more could co-operate, such as welfare of employees, or going deeper, the welfare of the country.

Other aims, admirable in themselves, such as welfare of wife and children, attract sympathy but would probably decline offers to share. One point stands out clearly, that if we face forward there are possibilities of finding aims which we can agree to pursue. If we look back and face the past we may find resemblances, but, the further we pursue the chains of causation which resulted in our coming together, the more these chains will be seen as distinct. While common suffering or common joy may be a basis for understanding and sympathy, they do not offer in themselves a basis for action. But if men with such common backgrounds looked forward, aims could be derived that two or more could agree upon. To know a man's history and reasons for his actions may help one to understand him. To know his aims enables one to hinder him or help him. The choice is always open.

If one is engaged in a transaction one may choose to help or to work for one's own ends. What happens to transactions when both parties choose to help? I suggest that each can adopt as his aim that the other should be better off as a result, and that each should be willing to transact further business. On these terms a transaction will be judged satisfactory if both sides are better off as a result and both are willing to continue to do business. This view of transactions may be extended to cover the interactions of members of a group, the difference being in this case that the members can have a joint aim. In terms of my proposed definition of transaction the effect of the operation of a group should be to increase its welfare and maintain the willingness of the members to continue together.

Enthusiasm is often one of the side effects of working in a group. I shall not attempt to explore the multitude of examples from history. Shared enthusiasm is very rewarding, but it is a poor end in itself, and is no guarantee that the activities round which it centres are either desirable (witness the enthusiasm of Nazis) or productive. Nevertheless enthusiasm can help men to face and overcome difficulties which would have daunted them without it. There is some evidence that the flame of enthusiasm can be usefully maintained in a group where there is a foreseeable end to its activities, but that where something unachievable has been undertaken, or where the task is endless, such as the maintenance of standards, the position changes. Possibly if a task is finite only a finite degree of involvement is called for, and if no end is envisaged then the relationship of being a member of a group is only possible with total involvement. So for practical purposes there may be much to be said for forming groups for limited objectives. When the objective is achieved the members may disperse, but one who has been a member of such a group becomes more easily a member of a fresh one.

Once the idea is accepted that one can be a useful member of a group without total involvement, the benefits of group formation for limited objectives become much more intelligible. The importance of comprehension and agreement remains, but, as with involvement, comprehension of and agreement about 'limited' objectives are much more accessible than about the unlimited or unachievable.

There is a question whether unanimity can be achieved voluntarily or whether groups have an insidious influence, in that there is pressure on individuals to conform, and that many people are susceptible to such pressure. Of course this can happen, and it is much more likely to happen if a man of seniority and high status in a group puts pressure on others. The greater the mutual trust and confidence, however, the less likely this is to happen.

Voluntary agreement or unanimity is desirable and where the social climate is such that men spontaneously choose to help each other, unanimity lacks the sour undertaste which may be detected in the term conformity.

I have been impressed by the effects on the deliberations and actions of groups where there is conscious concern among the members with aims and objectives, also by the way the realization that others share one's aims enhances mutual trust and reduces sparring for position. But, if men in such a group take their future in their hands and set out to mould it, it is of the utmost importance that they keep aspirations in mind as well as objectives. Getting on well together is one thing; doing a job well together is something different that doesn't follow automatically from the former.

Choosing to help is fundamental; it is the easier when looking forward shows us where aims are shared, but it is only the beginning. Once it is made, constructive work can begin. But making the choice does not tell you, any more than the commandment 'love your neighbour as yourself' tells you, what to do in practical terms. The meanings both of help and of love have to be discovered.

VII

HIGHER EDUCATION IN A TECHNOLOGICAL SOCIETY:

A STRATEGIC VIEW

Maurice Broady

The major strategic issue that will face higher education in the next twenty years concerns its relationship to the newly-developing technology and the social pressures which it will set up. Already, in what Clark Kerr has called the 'multiversity', i.e., the new-style American university, we can discern the start of this influence; and Clark Kerr himself, in his Godkin Lectures of 1963, gave the definitive blue-print of this kind of institution. The multiversity has been produced by the awareness, generated under the stimulus of the Second World War, that in a technological civilisation scientific knowledge is critical for social and economic progress. The main stimulus has been the investment of government money in particular aspects of university development: in 1960, the federal investment of $1 billion accounted for 75 per cent of all American university research expenditure. And the major effect has been to transform the role of the university from ivory-tower detachment to academic engagement in the surrounding society. With the development of what has been called the 'knowledge industry', the universities have become, in Kerr's words', 'the prime instrument of national purpose'.[1]

In a study which preceded this analysis by three years, Clark Kerr and his colleagues of the Department of Economics at Berkeley sought to delineate the pattern of organisation of the technologically-based society into which we were moving.[2] They argued, in that materialistic way to which tough-minded economists are prone, that in the long run the logic of economic growth would necessitate the development of a complementary structure of social organisation which they designated 'pluralistic industrialism'. In this type of society, authority would be concentrated in

---

[1] Clark Kerr, *The Uses of the University* (Harvard University Press, 1963), p. 87.
[2] *Industrialism and Industrial Man* by C. Kerr, J. T. Dunlop, F. H. Harbison, and C. A. Myers (Harvard University Press, 1960).

the hands of the state, the industrial enterprise and the professional association which would jointly elaborate a 'web of rules' to which 'industrial man' would be obliged to conform. Ideology would remain dead; conflict would focus increasingly upon administrative detail and less upon political principle (which would be rendered redundant by society's subservience to the logic of economic growth); and the loss of personal freedom at work and in political life would be balanced by the wider opportunities for leisure which the new technology would facilitate. The new technology and the logic of economic development would outweigh cultures and political philosophies in determining the pattern of social organisation; so that all industrial societies—the Soviet Union and the U.S.A. alike—would ultimately conform to one social type.

The argument is interesting and provocative: and there seem good grounds for supposing that, in an increasingly inter-related world, some common processes of this kind are likely to be at work in all our various countries. If we can make that initial assumption, then the major question is: how are these technological pressures likely to affect our university system? Clark Kerr's multiversity is perhaps the paradigm case. For both studies extrapolate from trends that are discernible particularly clearly in post-war California, whose meteoric economic growth has been based as much upon an advanced twentieth-century technology as upon its beneficent climate.

The most significant feature of the multiversity has been its changing relationship with the wider society. The point is made succinctly in Clark Kerr's use of the term 'the knowledge industry', as well as in his observations that 'the campus and society are undergoing a somewhat reluctant and cautious merger, already well advanced', and that 'the university and segments of industry are becoming more alike'.[3] Thus, not only are different countries, in Clark Kerr's view, becoming increasingly alike under the impact of the new technology, but within each society there is developing a kind of institutional convergence which directly affects the institutions of higher education.

Such convergence is not necessarily objectionable. Universities are and always have been part of their society and are inevitably related to it one way or another. But the notion of convergence

[3] Op. cit., pp. 115, 90.

masks the question of the relative influence of university and society in the 'somewhat reluctant and cautious merger' which they are experiencing. In the United States, there seems little doubt that the external factors are predominant and that the university is defensively accommodating itself to those pressures. For as the critiques with which I shall presently deal make clear, higher education is regarded both by the government and by the student as primarily an investment, and a university degree as a path to power and a means to increased socio-economic well-being.

The growth of interest in education in Great Britain in the last few years has also been based upon a similarly instrumental conception. 'The nation's economic future depends on education', cried a recent campaign to improve education, sensitive to the point that a nation of shopkeepers is best tackled through its pockets, and a similar view of education has been written into every recent governmental pronouncement on the universities. The language of education no longer uses the organic metaphor of growth but speaks instead in the mechanistic concepts of industrial production. We are apt nowadays to speak of improving 'teaching productivity', to think of graduates as 'output', to conceive efficiency in terms of a simple ratio between intake and output. And the government undermines the autonomy of the universities by the policy of the binary system,[4] administering the technical colleges in a way that makes them more biddable to pragmatic ends, by deflating the University Grants Committee, the remarkable buffer between the universities and government, and by making universities' accounts open to government inspection. In short, in Britain too, the universities are being increasingly influenced by external factors that derive from new technology and a growing governmental interest in higher education.

One can only speculate on the significance of these changes for the future of the British university. But the American case—and notably that of Berkeley—gives us a clear indication of one possible line of development. Certainly, the Berkeley affair[5] is very complex: but certain major features can be discerned. The Considine report which the Berkeley faculty produced last year

[4] By which the universities are handled by a different administrative pattern to that concerned with the colleges of further education.
[5] For description and comments see: *Berkeley, the New Student Revolt* by H. Draper (Grove Press, New York, 1965); *The Berkeley Student Revolt* ed. S. M. Lipset and S. S. Wolin (Doubleday Anchor, New York, 1965).

in an attempt to decide what had gone wrong with education at Berkeley, made the general point: 'The actual operation of our system is sometimes quite contrary to the intention, and seems more preoccupied with the administration rather than the education of the student: . . . The overall thrust of the system (of degrees), particularly outside the sciences, can be to discourage intellectual curiosity, *self*-motivation and playful curiosity'. In proposing reforms of the grading system, the report comments that 'Above all, it would de-emphasise the system itself, and thus create an academic milieu with greater freedom, diversity, leisure and personally-motivated inquiry'.[6] In short, the system was too rigid. The rigidity of the courses; the focus on an objective grading system; the repetitive examinations; the devaluation of teaching and neglect of students; the absentee professor engaged in research and consultancy and allocating the training of students to low-grade assistants: these are the characteristics of a dehumanised educational system geared to thinking in purely *external* terms of universities as machines rather than as organic communities—characteristics of a system which, as Clark Kerr himself remarked, though apparently without appreciating the significance of the point, had accommodated to changing social circumstances without much positive thought.[7]

The atmosphere of a university to which the Considine report refers is affected chiefly by the pedagogical assumptions to which the university is committed. Here again the mechanistic assumptions of American higher education have been called in question. The distinction between training and education has been largely muffed and intellectual activity reduced to learning 'an *amount* of information and ideas'. In a striking critique by Carl Rodgers, of the assumptions held by a large and important department of psychology, several clusters of attitudes can be discerned.[8] There is, first, of all, an approach to knowledge:

> (1) *method* is science (ii) the truths of psychology are known (iii) knowledge is the accumulation of brick upon brick of content and information and (iv) what is presented in the lecture is what the student learns.

[6] *Education at Berkeley*, Report of the Select Committee on Education (University of California, Berkeley, March, 1966), pp. 167, 99.
[7] Kerr, *op. cit.*, pp. 49, 56.
[8] Carl R. Rodgers, 'Graduate Education in Psychology: a Passionate Statement' (mimeographed article, 1964). Professor Rodgers was at the time on the faculty of the University of Wisconsin.

Second, an attitude to the student:
> (i) students are best regarded as manipulable objects, not persons (ii) they cannot be trusted to pursue their own scientific and professional learning, and (iii) creative scientists develop from passive learners.

Third, attitudes to assessment:
> (i) evaluation is education and education is evaluation, (ii) ability to pass exams is the best criterion for judging student promise, and (iii) 'weeding out' a majority of the students is a satisfactory method of producing scientists and clinicians.

That which distinguishes a technological outlook or ideology from its antithesis is not the desire to plan rationally to secure future goals. The distinction is rather one that centres around an awareness of the autonomy of human beings and an acknowledgement of the importance of human beings in social affairs. It is a question of the context of assumptions within which planning—be it of an economy or of a curriculum—is carried out. The technological ideology supposes that there are in principle no limitations to what can be achieved by rational means. It is therefore insensitive to the possibility of autonomous human activity: this disposition can be clearly seen running through the assumptions that Carl Rodgers has elicited.

As Rodgers makes clear, many psychologists know quite enough to criticize these assumptions. Their prevalence can only be explained by the power of academic fashions and the unwillingness or inability of academics independently to criticise their own assumptions.

Several recent commentaries on the effects of all this on American students show that the students' academic-professional interests are not integrated with his personal concerns, and that therefore his education merely serves to emphasise the duality. Kenneth Keniston picks out the schism between public performance and private meaning as the salient features of the modern American student.[9] 'Learning,' says J. L. Stewart does not 'take hold' because it is not internalised, because 'the students don't see much of the education they are receiving as having any significant

---

[9] K. Keniston, 'Faces in the Lecture Room', *Yale Alumni Magazine*, April, 1966. Professor Keniston teaches psychology at Yale.

relation to or relevance for deepest human concern.[10] As Keniston goes on to argue, the present-day American student has about him all the marks of the professional man: 'intense technical competence, high professional expertise, and careful specialisation'—but, on the other side, 'often disappointingly unwilling to become excited about ideas . . . (unable) to afford the luxury of enthusiasm when the next admissions office is only around the corner.'[11] Disinclined to consider wider ideas, and frequently quite unable to find in his private life the justification for his public, professional activities, the student can find no independent intellectual pied-à-terre from which to make an independent assessment of the professional ethos to which he is committed: so that even the protesters settle down to conformity.

Certainly, this cannot all be charged simply to the universities. The students are what they are already because of assumptions made and social pressures enforced by the wider society. 'The divorce of public from private (says Keniston) reflects all-too-faithfully the demands of our technological society, which expects of its responsible citizens extraordinary objectivity, impersonality, competence, control and cognitive efficiency; and leaves little room in public life for private commitment, idealism, passions, zeal, indignation and feeling'.[12] The universities are bound to be influenced by the general tenor of social life, since they are part of society and supported by it and therefore unlikely ever to be permitted an absolute freedom. But one sees the universities, no doubt with the best of intentions, accommodating themselves like prostrating priests to the demands and the assumptions of their society, without a critical assessment of what is involved for the intellectual development which is their chief vocation. The present-day assumption of American, and I have no doubt of many European, academics is that the university's social function is fulfilled by producing 'millions of well-trained, technically-competent and professionally-skilled young men and women to man the American economy'. Keniston wishes to see as equally necessary 'men and women *with a capacity for critical detachment*

---

[10] J. L. Stewart, 'Education for Leisure', in *The New Challenge in Lifelong learning. A conference on the future role of the University in relation to Public Service*, California University: Senate Committee on University Extension, 1965, p. 57. Professor Stewart is on the Faculty of the Humanities Dept., University of California—San Diego.

[11] Keniston, op. cit., pp. 23, 25.

[12] Keniston, op. cit., p. 33.

from their communities, a sense of ethics above traditional piety, a capacity to articulate new goals, and a sustained determination to work towards the realization of those goals'. The university should be in brief, 'a countervailing centre of the *immediate* trends of society'.[13] Its function,[14] as Alec Vidler once put it, should be 'to sow the seeds of scepticism in an all-too-credulous society'.

In Britain, Duncan Davies of ICI has criticised the effect of British university education in dampening curiosity and innovation.[15] Similarly, the inadequacy of the older pattern of mechanical mathematics taught in British schools and deriving from a period when the major demand was for competent book-keepers, has been found inadequate to the demands of a technological society and a 'new maths' has been developed which is designed to encourage the student to *understand for himself* what he is doing. Industry —engineering for example—is beginning to appreciate the importance of training people to think creatively, precisely because it is upon this that innovation depends and because with the vast rate at which scientific knowledge accummulates, only the autonomous person can accommodate effectively to change. My point is, therefore, that it is coming to be appreciated that an education that dampens autonomy is dysfunctional in a highly advanced society.

One may retain doubts about the speed with which university authorities, unconcerned with pedagogy as they tend to be, will adapt to these demands. One has the sense that, in Britain at least, we may be straining everything to produce a mass educational system of the American pattern, and that we shall have produced it without noting the fact that the Americans have changed their practice to meet new circumstances. Be that as it may, a second trend away from a dehumanised, technocratic education can be seen in two respects in student preferences.

First of all, there appears to be evidence for the view that students are disinclined, both in Britain and the United States, to choose a career in industry. At least in the U.S.A. a sizeable minority of the present generation seems inclined to rebel against the cliché that young people are a national economic asset and to

[13] Ibid., p. 34.
[14] Commemoration address, Southampton University, 1962.
[15] D. Davies, 'A scarce resource called curiosity', *The Listener*, 4 May 1967.

repudiate a vocation between whose purposes and their own they can see no connection.[16]

Second, there is the interesting phenomenon, in Britain and evidently in other advanced industrial nations as well, that students are swinging away from the physical sciences in their choice of a university course, in favour of the humanities, psychology, sociology and medicine. Whereas in 1961, 43 per cent of first year sixth-formers opted for science, in 1970 the proportion —on present trends—could be as low as 23 per cent.[17] This is particularly interesting given that it is considerably easier to get into the science and engineering faculties of British universities than into the arts or social sciences. This curious phenomenon means that the national demand for an increase of scientists and technologists is being frustrated by personal choice. It is interesting that the explanations which have been advanced by the academic planners are couched in terms of 'objective' characteristics, first of the students themselves, then of the regime through which they have passed. It is suggested that the calibre of teaching is lower in science than in the humanities, and secondly, that our students feel that 'technology and the physical sciences have outrun man's understanding of man and his capacity to make proper use of modern discoveries and inventions'.[18] One might suggest as a rather more profound reason that many students are increasingly unwilling to commit themselves to a course in the natural sciences which appears likely to force them into an impersonal mould, and seek in these other fields the opportunity of studying something which will not only have a professional value but will also—so they perhaps falsely believe—help them *as persons* to understand themselves.

A third phenomenon is, of course, the revival in the last few years of a new and critical spirit in the universities, notably at Berkeley but also more recently in London at the School of Economics, in Strasbourg, Berlin and Milan. The causes of

[16] 'Is Business letting young people down?' *The Harvard Business Review*, Nov.-Dec., 1965, quoted in A. D. Bonham-Carter, 'U.K. Industry and the Universities—Are they in Step?' *Progress*, vol. 290, 1966. Some British evidence is also quoted. See also, A. Newsome, 'The Appointments Board: a window on two worlds', *Progress*, vol. 52, no. 1 (1967).

[17] Report of *The Observer*, 4th June, 1967, of a speech by the Vice-Chancellor of Nottingham University at a Royal Society Symposium on Scientific Manpower.

[18] *The Observer*, loc. cit.

these movements and their interrelation require fuller and closer investigation, but in Berkeley, and I imagine the same to be valid elsewhere, a great deal can be explained by reference to the difference between the student generation of the 1950's and the present 'Kennedy generation'. This is, as the reports on Berkeley make clear, a generation that has grown to maturity in the era of the civil rights movement and the idealism of Voluntary Service Overseas, inspired by the fusion of intellect and humanity that marked the Kennedy presidency. In the case of Berkeley, at least, it is well-established that it was the intellectually more able who constituted the core of the Free Speech movement. And the fact that it finally secured the broad support of the faculty and students and teaching assistants indicates that, whatever political factors were involved, there were genuine grievances against the academic system. The Berkeley revolt can be reasonably interpreted as the assertion by the students of a claim not to be pressed by a university, of which so much more was to be expected, into a mould of economically useful conformity to their professions and to the prevailing political outlook. They were asserting that they were also—perhaps primarily—*persons*, human beings with wills and minds of their own, moral agents with concerns and a responsibility wider than that of their careers, able and anxious to appraise and criticise what they were being offered in the university and in the wider political world, of which—as they saw it—the university was becoming a far too conforming microcosm.

If this is a valid interpretation, then the central strategic problem which faces us in the universities is that of defending, against external pressures to conformity, both the independence of universities themselves and the personal counterpart to that— the autonomy of students within them. It will be argued that the future of our societies and the immediate needs of our economy are dependent upon the universities. Conformity to these demands will be congenial to many a Vice-Chancellor dependent upon government finance, to many a lecturer and many a student intent upon their careers. But the university must have a broader outlook. It does not do its job simply by adjusting to the alleged needs of society. Its task is best fulfilled by injecting a tension into the life around: only in that way is anything new and creative likely to be generated.

We need a fuller elaboration of a university's proper relation-

I

ship to society. As Galbraith has pointed out, 'the rich society continues to assume that economic condition must be the dominant influence on social thought and action'.[19] In general, he continues, our national policies 'remain under the spell of economic compulsion' long after individuals have escaped from such preoccupation. Thus, the very economic development that allows the expansion of higher education also permits a greater freedom rather than a greater dependence upon economic considerations.

I believe that this greater freedom is showing itself in Britain, for example, not only in the revival of the arts but also in the growth of voluntary agencies and pressure group politics. And this is understandable. Economic advance demands more advanced education, and education at that level is not only a training for a job but also an introduction to democratic practice. No wonder that in Berkeley it was precisely the more capable students who were in the lead of revolt. It accords well enough with the sociological generalisation that it is not those who are most oppressed, but those who can see *both* the oppression and the possibilities of emancipation who lead revolutions. Accordingly, one has reason to call in question Clark Kerr's simplistic view of leisure as a palliative for an increasingly enslaved 'industrial man'.

An alternative view of the nature of the technological future is that advanced recently by Radovan Richta of Prague, whose work emphasises the scientific-cum-technological aspects of the change. 'The basic law of the development of the forces of production under the conditions of the scientific-technological revolution is the absolute priority of science over technology and technology over direct production. Here we come up against new kinds of relationship which were unknown in the industrial revolution. It is not a matter of satisfying man's material needs more effectively by technological development but of changing the place of man in the world of productive forces, of freeing him from compulsory division of labour, of overcoming the self-alienation of man, of his fulfilling his own nature (what it is in him to be)—to be a creator on earth'.[20] What a contrast between this conception of man and that of Kerr and his colleagues! For what Kerr is offering,

---

[19] J. K. Galbraith. 'Economics *v* the Quality of Life', *Encounter*, vol. 24, no. 1 (January, 1965), p. 31.

[20] Translated from 'Kann die Zukunft geplant werden?'—a synopsis of the ideas of Professor Richta and his colleagues, presented at a conference convened by the Kammer für Arbeiter und Angestellter der Stadt Wien, April, 1967.

socially, is a leisure which is nothing more than another form of alienation.

Now if this view of the new reality is valid, then we need to attune our educational system to the requirements of personal autonomy: we should seek to encourage the student to develop his abilities rather than dampen them. The usual way of thinking about the institutional implications of university growth is to think of these as governed by broad national considerations relating to finance, numbers and the rest—all the factors external to the process of education *per se*. It is this approach which produced Berkeley. It is this approach which leads to talk of educational efficiency measured crudely in terms of an input-output relationship: a view which would accept the failure rate as an adequate index of efficiency, ignoring the fact that efficiency is also a function of the effort and interest and understanding that can be aroused in the student. The technocratic view of education ignores the salient point that education, to be efficient, requires the collaboration of the student. Efficiency is now secured by piling on the work, by putting the student under the duress of examinations: by all the methods which Carl Rodgers was criticising in his paper —i.e. by *external* constraints; or by the hope that good, intelligent students will come through despite the constraints. What must be criticised is the gross imbalance in educational thinking between this and the idea of encouragement or inducement. 'Why is it (asks Rodgers) . . . that a faculty member who fails half his students on an examination is likely to be regarded as a better, because more 'tough-minded', instructor than his colleague who fails none?'[21]

It is this 'objective' view that leads, I believe, to the under-valuation of teaching. If teaching is nothing more than conveying an amount of information and ideas as the teaching-machine boys appear to believe,[22] then clearly no other techniquest han reading from the book are in order. But these theories seem to ignore the fact that understanding is more than having information and ideas: it is rather to have incorporated such ideas and information into one's known personality, so that they can be used to personal ends. That is the aim of the teacher, a quite distinctive one, one which

[21] C. Rodgers, op. cit., p. 14.
[22] B. Hopson, 'Modernising University Teaching', *New Society*, No. 218 (1st December, 1966), p. 827.

could be the starting point for this 'new paradigm for effective teachers' for which J. L. Stewart calls.[23]

Clearly, the central point of all this is pedagogical. It is understandable that pedagogy is held by academics in such low esteem. Not only is it far less a source of prestige than 'scientific work', it also smacks of the merely technical. In fact, of course, a pedagogy implies a total view of the world and one's activities: it is a philosophy which involves normative moral judgements; and it is, I suspect, an aspect of the technological, positivistic emphasis of the modern academic that this kind of thing is not taken seriously. Precisely because, in Britain at least, the academic profession itself fails to take seriously what is meant by pedagogy, it becomes possible for the internal conduct of universities to be directly affected from outside.

In conclusion, therefore, but as a start for your discussion, I wish to insist on pedagogy and to put forward a point of view about the purpose of teaching.

There are two broad approaches to knowledge, and to the communicating of an academic discipline, which I shall designate as 'the subject approach' and 'the argument approach'. For the most part, academic disciplines are taught as 'subjects'. To speak of subjects implies some kind of classification of knowledge, which exists objectively, independently of the student. History for example, conceived as a subject, has a beginning and an end; it is a determinate thing impersonal and external. It is cut out of the knowable, already established and set within clear boundaries. 'Is this sociology or is it *really* history?' they ask. Appropriately enough, the pedagogy that relates to this conception is that of *subjecting* students to knowledge. The student is seen as an empty bucket which must be filled up with knowledge—'the purpose of the second year (as a colleague said to me recently) is to pump in the facts'; and the role of the teacher becomes that of a man shovelling knowledge into the students' bucket, in a total system in which the teacher is the authority and the student a passive recipient of wisdom.

This is the layman's view of intellectual activity: understandably so, since he has for the most part been so taught. But those of us who make knowledge, who are concerned professionally with it, are aware that the image is wrong. What we are doing as

[23] J. L. Stewart, op. cit., p. 60.

academics is to engage in arguments. Notice the significance of the verb: to argue. It is something that *I* do; it is *my* argument, not *that* subject. It is something, therefore, that more readily permits of human participation, in an active sense. Furthermore, whereas the conception of a subject entails a concern for the objective limits of each kind of knowledge, the conception of argument leads more readily to the question: 'where is it driving?' 'what is the point of the argument?' 'what constitutes relevance for this argument?' and is thus more purposive and flexible. Regarded sociologically, the idea of argument implies a mutuality, a common interest uniting divergent opinions in which the academic and his student are in principle equals. It goes less well with the image of the autocratic professor than with the image of scholarship as an active interchange of subjective opinions, in which *we* are involved collaboratively in an effort to see which opinion can be more convincingly validated by reference to objective data.

Clearly, these are ideal types. But I prefer the concept of argument since, among other things, it more closely approximates to what one actually does, to how one practices the craft of scholarship. We are often prone to distort reality by conforming to academic fashions. In a recent article, Professor P. B. Medawar[24] refers to the 'fraud of the scientific paper', with its carefully elaborated form of discussion of the literature, methods, findings, etc.; this quite misrepresents the much more confused and intuitive nature of scientific inquiry. The same applies, I believe, to a pedagogy that sees knowledge entirely as a subject and not as an argument. It is this disposition which is likely to be fostered, not directly by the rational planning of universities but by the technocratic emphasis currently associated with it. The demands of the Berkeley students make sense. The salient problem of a university in a technological society is the need to safeguard and foster the independence of its academics and the autonomy of its students.

[24] P. J. Medawar, 'Is the Scientific Paper a Fraud', *The Listener*, vol. 70, no. 1798 (12th September, 1963).

VIII

A CONTRIBUTION TO THE CLIMATE OF OPINION ON SEXUAL MORES

JOSEPHINE KLEIN

It may be thought that everything that needs to be said on the moral theology of sexual relations has already been said. Certainly many alternative views have been stated, and are every now and then debated, by the highly educated. The highly educated, with all this implies in terms of ignorance about how others live, have highly educated views on the significance of sexual relationships and these we publish in pamphlets and booklets and books. Some interesting points remain to be made, however, at a practical level.

I have lately had some contact with a set of people between 15 and 25 who by many criteria could be called emotionally and socially deprived, and the present paper is the result of reflections upon this contact. There is no evidence to suggest that the people I met are markedly more deprived than the normal population, with two reservations, one of which may not be of great significance. They differ from the normal population in that rather a large proportion spent their early years in orphanages and other such institutions, and in that many are unemployed or casually employed. Many are 'dropouts'; it is however a moot point how far this can be considered evidence of major psychological disturbance, causally. It is a tenable view, and I am inclined to it, that they are representative of the total population except insofar as they are not resigned to the lives they would lead had they not dropped out. Incidentally, all socio-economic groups (judged by parental occupation) seem to be represented in roughly the pyramidical shape which the total social structure of this country displays.

I stress the possible representativeness of this group of people because what follows may present a major temptation to this audience, and others, to argue that I am referring only to the needs of a small minority.

What is unrepresentative about this group is not that they don't like the paid work that they might be doing (very few people like their employment) nor that they don't like the family life they might be leading (few people have found in their family a vivid source of happiness) but that they avoid work and family, and vote with their feet for being cold, hungry, ill clad and the object of general casual social disapproval. In a rather ineffective way they hang about on the fringes of the illegal. They are often depressed. Again I should stress that there is nothing abnormal or unrepresentative about being depressed, except that their depression is shown by at times lying about looking miserable, at times taking refuge in drink, any drugs that can be obtained, or, if they are feeling somewhat better, any sex that they can obtain, or if capable of showing aggression, maybe a fight. I may mention other ways of living through depressions, like playing squash, going to the pictures, watching TV, dozing by the fire, etc. Depressions are normal, and there is a variety of ways of living through them.

Maybe at this point I should state my general view, which is that most people live way below their capacity for living. Most people are most of the time emotionally and socially under-employed, deprived if you like. If this is so, and if, for whatever reason, one has a concern for others, where is one to start amending? One starting point is with those who are frequently confronted with the fact that their situation is dire. It is an easy starting point.

This lengthy preamble serves to introduce another set of people (for convenience I will refer to them as the 'agency') in whom I have been taking an interest. It is their rationale and their views on what for convenience I will refer to as the 'clientele' which I have been sketching out above—it is different from the usual social work one.

Here is the point at which the argument proper begins. *This agency finds it impossible to co-operate fully with any of the statutory or voluntary social work agencies (including concerned people from the churches) who find that they have a concern for this clientele.* It is difficult to co-operate with them informally, and impossible to do so officially.

It may be that the general reason is that the others think, or in their working hours think, that the feelings of the clientele in which they take an interest are basically different from their own: that they themselves are never depressed, never indulge in unrealistic dreams, live fully. This is a difficult one to discuss, because in talking about it, people very very quickly say: 'Ah well, we're all sinners; of course we're all neurotic, etc., etc.,' and in a sense they mean it and know it, but they don't mean it and know it in their working hours, when it is relevant.

There is however a convenient test case, and that is about sex. The clientele showed all kinds of sexual patterns: total abstinence and lack of interest, total abstinence with fears attached, a rather low-drive sexual opportunism, varied and frequent promiscuous sex, sex with a steady, or mainly with a steady, for periods up to say six months. How do the usual social work agencies react to this?

Words and expressed opinions don't matter; let us be yet more concrete. Since a number of the clientele are homeless, or practically homeless, the reaction of many who come in contact with them is to find them somewhere to live. It is not my purpose to argue the merit of this, though in London, where there is a good deal of exploitation, the case for inexpensive hostels seems to me very very strong.

The question is, what are to be the sexual mores of the hostel? No existing agency thinking of running a hostel, as far as I know, would consider tolerating short-term liaisons in the hostel, for any reason whatever. My contention is that good reasons exist, though the main part of this paper is to demolish bad reasons. Why should such liaisons not be tolerated? We will assume that our interlocutor is thinking out his position as he goes along. A first answer might be in terms of public opinion, worries about adverse press publicity, unfavourable notice from the police, from other local authorities, from local residents and, for sure, from paid and unpaid religious functionaries. This is an expediential, not a moral objection. It could be that public opinion is unenlightened, mistaken, or morally wrong. If so, it ought to be a matter of moral importance to put better thoughts before the public. Hereupon our interlocutor may attempt something on the lines of 'marriage is a sacred institution' and needs to be reminded that marriage is not under discussion, and that a hostel such as is under discussion impairs the institution of marriage less than did, for instance, the rules of Kent County Council, and no doubt of others in this country, who provide hostels, not for homeless families, but for wives and children only, compelling husbands to live elsewhere. This is so extraordinary that I must devote some moments to make the matter clear. The husbands are not permitted to stay the night. This means that at a time of crisis like being without a family-home, the husband is made to desert his family, to live apart in lodgings, earning his living by day, searching for a home in his spare time and dropping in on his family in spare moments. After three months of this, the mothers are also expelled from the hostel; the children can then be taken into institutional care without the parents' consent, if they have nowhere to go. The scandal of King Hill gained some publicity around Christmas 1965 because due process of law jailed some of the men when they refused to leave their wives, who refused to leave the hostel when their three months were up.[1]

Looking through these records one finds again that tendency of those in contact with people in obvious need to lose all sense of common humanity. A Police Inspector calls parents scum at a children's party, in front of the children. Mr. Justice Lawton, who jailed the men, points out to them that they are no worse off than soldiers separated from their families. Kent County Councillors call them trouble-makers. Dr. Elliott, then Kent Medical Officer of Health, refers several times to the criminal tendencies of the men who want to stay with their families. I should add, in passing, that of the 269 families admitted to this hostel in 1964, only six per cent were homeless because of eviction for non-payment of rent.

From 'Marriage is a Sacred Institution' our interlocutor may go on to reformulate his worries in terms of theology, saying 'man and wife are one flesh'. If at this moment we point out that we are not talking about men and their wives, we arrive at our interlocutor's feeling that sexual intercourse has a mystical significance such that the first act of sexual intercourse is the one that counts in the eyes of a god who has so arranged matters that . . . . I don't know what, we don't know what, but an unexamined feeling remains that the first act counts in a way for which there is no biblical evidence whatsoever.

Already in these preliminary skirmishes it is noticeable that our interlocutor is assuming that the people under consideration are already malign and that it would be best for all if they would look

---

[1] The unbearable story is summarized in *KCC versus the Homeless* printed by the Radical Press, 3a Highgate Road, London, N.W.4.

for a marriage-partner. Indeed most arguments normally classified as liberal on matters of sex assume this, and consider special cases of highly responsible reflective people who might or might not justifiably engage in sexual intercourse with those they are not married to. To this we shall return. But we should not leave the 'one flesh' argument without referring to one of those quibbles with which nature tends to confound the neater logical or theological categorizations. The quibble is, when does 'one flesh' become a fact? In Michael Schofield's sample of nearly a thousand boys and girls, over half the older boys (17–19) had experience of active genital stimulation and over a third had experience of genital apposition without full sexual intercourse; the corresponding proportions for girls were just slightly lower in each case. And early attempts at full sexual intercourse may be so fumbling and confused, as to make the one flesh notion absurd. Less than a third of the girls, less than half the boys, who had engaged in sexual intercourse, had liked their first experience of it.

One flesh?[2]

Our interlocutor now turns to more general ideas about what is right and what is wrong, and being that sort of person, he turns to the Gospels. The Gospels actually have rather little to say on sexual mores—more interestingly still, they have rather little to say about any mores, and are mainly concerned with living, loving, feeling, creating, suffering, healing and redeeming, and other such processes. Nevertheless, there are some disapprovals and condemnations attributed to Jesus. About these I wish to say two things: one concerns the Jewish lack of obsessiveness about sex, the other concerns our obsessiveness about sex. Jesus seems to have associated with all sorts of what we would now call social deviants and what were then called sinners, among whom tax collectors were especially prominent. People were generally disapproved of in that culture if they earned their money in certain ways, if they allied themselves with the *de facto* government, if they did not wash their hands before meals, or did not pay their priesthood. There is remarkably little reference to *people* engaged in sexual misdemeanours, though adultery and fornication are condemned in general terms (rather less than social injustice, however, if a content analysis were made).

[2] M. Schofield, *The Sexual Behaviour of Young People* (Longman's, 1965), pp. 28 and 65.

Contemporary Christians, on the other hand, especially those with a concern for others, worry first and foremost about sexual behaviour among any kind of social-work clientele, with men's long hair coming a close second. (I mean they worry in a moral kind of way, not that they try to understand the psychological implications of sexual behaviour). You do not see them with that characteristic anxious frown waiting for the first opportunity to tell rich people they ought to consider the use of their money, to tell censorious people they ought to get the beam out of their eyes, or to tell little old poor ladies they ought not to be so attached to their few possessions. They are more patient and tolerant in these cases, understanding more easily the circumstances which lead to such behaviour and the difficulties in the way of abandoning it.

The Epistles, written by Jesus' early followers, are somewhat different from the Gospels in this matter. Revolutionary movements tend to attract the more way-out people, and the writers of the Epistles seem to have been both more vociferously communistic and to have more of a thing about sex.

The fact remains that Christian and post-Christian social workers of whatever description have on their committees people who offend against the Gospel way of life in one way or another, but that nevertheless they cannot engage in any activity which allows them to let their clientele fornicate.

I now wish to turn to another stumbling block to the clear consideration of how our imaginary hostel should be run, and that is, that the clientele are so obviously irresponsible about interpersonal commitments. I have already alluded to the fact that what are called liberal views on sexual matters, Christian and other, are concerned with responsible people, responsible sex, deep serious attachments, careful consideration. With regard to those not capable of this there is silence where there is not condemnation. The reason is clear, for it touches us all, and it is painful to think developmentally about the gaps in our own development. Very few of the writers give away the fact that they have interpersonal and sexual difficulties of their own, with which they would wish to be grappling in order to get on better. I have already referred to the tendency if you are doing social work with people with problems, to assume, at least during working hours, that you have no problems.

The result is that everyone who is judged not capable of responsibility is assumed capable of chastity, and if necessary has to have chastity imposed on him, like prayer went with soup in the nineteenth century. Worse, everybody who is not mature has to sit about till somehow maturity comes to them. There is nothing developmental about these notions: you're either mature or you aren't, except perhaps for another unexamined notion, which is that once people are 'saved' and/or praying and/or receiving Holy Communion regularly and devoutly, they become mature. Even this, I am prepared to speculate, even this might be the case, if there were any guidance, any developmental notions about the progressive practice of salvation, prayer or sacrament. But this guidance is inaccessible to all but the most minuscule proportion of the population of the U.K. In short, and more with-it language, 'man, it's a con'.

It's a con. We take girls whose immaturity is demonstrated by the fact that at 20 they have had three children by three different fathers, and establish hostels for them, from which we pretend they can leave to make a good marriage. Or we put them in touch again with the families they ran away from five years ago. We take young men whose immaturity shows itself in the fact that they willingly live with a lot of other young men in a hostel, during which time their heterosexual encounters can only take place under bushes or in doorways, and we ignore the fact that tramps over 40 have just such a history behind them. Where would they ever learn to get on with a relaxed girl, where would they learn to relax with a girl? To pray with them, for them, over them, is no more to the point than praying for the economic crisis to go away. The best that can happen to them is that they will become like the people who do this to them.

The world just is not constructed in this way. What can be said about the world as it is? The basic premise is that our society is not a traditional one perpetuating itself without much change from generation to generation. Everyone is at least aware of the opportunities for change in the social structure. This means that people cannot learn the complex but clearly defined roles which make for personal satisfaction and feelings of worth in a traditional society. If they do conform to those roles, they easily feel that they are missing out on something, that others less careful to go by conventional routes are getting better pay-offs, either materially or in other forms of personal worth. They may indeed be mistaken about this, but it is a general feeling. Certainly I go on the assumption, which would need justification in another paper, that feelings of worth must in a changing society derive from a personality that can freely move in the world as it is, that feelings of worth can no longer derive from a set of well-learned roles well performed. Epigrammatically, now people must become persons before they can take on roles, whereas in a traditional society people become persons by learning the roles.

In social situations where you don't know what is expected of you, or where you don't know what you want to do, or where what is expected of you is not what you have learnt to want, you tend to lose your bearings, you don't feel real, the situation appears meaningless—you are experiencing a crisis of identity, you feel nullified, life feels futile.

To bring us back to the point, let me summarize a picture of life that was felt to be rewarding by many at the turn of the century, and which is now felt by many to be stultifying: *A man with a sufficient income to furnish a house and support a wife and children meets, falls in love with and marries a girl willing to settle down as housewife, mother, hostess. Previous experience of adult human contact on either side: the office, the theatre bar, dances, family visits.*

What else is there to living? It is too early to tell, but it is possible to sketch out some of the tasks which have to be learnt, if possible during adolescence, if people are to have an adult sense of their own personal worth and that of others. There is nothing new, perhaps, about the tasks; what is undoubtedly true is that they cannot now be learned by learning a set of roles once and for all.

What do boys and girls learn, when they learn to get on with each other? I mention a brief list, to point the direction in which our thinking might go, and by thinking, remember, I mean 'moral theology' here. Any moral theology would need either to accept that these tasks have to be learned, or to deny it, and would need either to accept that to attempt these tasks in all spheres except the sexual is futile, or to deny that.

For the purposes of this paper I do not need to dwell on the difficulties many experience, at one time or another, in getting their bodies to behave in accordance with their fantasies, and failure can be a deeply wounding experience. Promiscuity, in that it enables the unsuccessful partners to try more successfully elsewhere, is a short-term solution for some, simply because more successful experiences build up confidence and skill. Others carry their humiliation for years, even for life. It is of course a short-term solution, because the hunt for a good orgasm is an inward-turning narcissistic pursuit, which does not in itself enable people to understand themselves or other people. In other words, it does not fit them to survive with a feeling of personal value. Not on its own, and there are all the wounded to think of.

Here are other things which need to be learnt, and which can only be learned in interaction. The first discovery when a girl and a boy meet in an adult way is that the other really is 'other'. Well, maybe not the first. There may first be the entrancing discovery of common ground. But the point comes when each must acknowledge the real existence of the other person, as really other, and if they can't take it, they part, perhaps on realistic grounds, perhaps because they cannot yet give up the wish to have others as an extension of themselves. But if they don't part, they have also discovered, at least in one instance, that relationships with others are possible, even if they are 'other'. It would be interesting, and I believe distressing, to survey how many adults contemporarily are capable of relating to those unlike themselves, and how many get progressively trapped into monotony, boredom and loneliness.

To go over this ground again, in interaction, people discover the difficulties in giving affection to another (by affection I mean more or less a conviction of personal worth) so that it is in effect experienced by the other as affection. And conversely, there is learning to receive affection in an enhancing affectionate way. To go over the same ground again, in interaction people learn how to cope with the anger of depression which results from the discovery of otherness. A list like this could go on a while, but I will leave it for anyone to elaborate it in his own language, mentioning only one other task, among the many. The pair learns that it must relate to larger groupings if narcissistic obsessiveness and boredom are not to slay them, and they must learn how to do this.

I have mentioned some of the extraordinarily difficult tasks which need to be learnt in a social situation where role-learning does not create self-hood. And I have put forward some considerations which would need to be taken into account by those who wish to write moral theology about sex. I will end on an optimistic expediential note.

The irritating thing about all this is that there is now a good technology about how to help people, thought out by the better social workers of the recent generation. All the equipment is there, *except* the moral climate which would enable them to get on with it. Basically, help consists in talking with people about a recent experience so that its full meaning can be felt and evaluated. People then begin to ask themselves classic questions: 'Is this what I wanted'? In which direction do I want to go? 'How do I think I'll get along faster?' 'What's hindering me?' 'What do I propose to do about it?' 'Was that a successful attempt to clear something up?' But at the moment this is not possible, and agencies who attempt anything like it have to fight constant battles with those with whom they should be co-operating. For this we must all bear the blame, for in this profoundly important aspect of living, nothing to the point has been said by the leaders of opinion for the last two thousand years.

IX

GOAL LANGUAGE AND VISION LANGUAGE IN THEOLOGY

A. E. HILLS

i

In this paper I intend to do three things. First, I shall try to make clear a number of distinctions within the language we use when we conceive and put into practice our plans for the future. I shall distinguish chiefly between what I shall call 'goal' and 'vision' language, and the discussion of this will form the centre of the paper. Second, I shall suggest that these distinctions have a clear relevance to the interpretation of the theological idea of 'the Logos'. And third, I shall make one or two points about the relationship of the behavioural sciences and theology in the light of the arguments developed in the paper.

This approach was suggested by two considerations arising from the Conference. The first is a general one, concerning the nature of theology and its status as a discipline comparable to, e.g., sociology. The days when theology was 'queen of the sciences' and had a subject matter all its own are past, and theologians seem to be turning to such fields as sociology or politics or psychiatry in an attempt to find a point of relevance and certainty from which to speak. This crisis in the subject matter of theology has reached a climax in the 'death of God' movement, but in fact theology has never relied wholly on 'religious' matters for its construction. It has always drawn upon the ideas and words, even the fundamental attitudes of the age in which it works, and if today the theologian comes to the scientist or writer with a rather less confident air than before, it is certainly not because he is doing something quite foreign to him. At a conference such as this the theologian would be obstinate who did not attempt to draw upon the resources opened to him in getting on with his constant task of confronting the documents and traditions of the church with the needs of the age.

This general hint as to a possible approach was given precision by the metaphor of the railway compartment in Mr. Babington-Smith's paper which he used to illustrate his call for a more future-orientated attitude in Social Science. That is, he believes social science should contain a stronger element of planning for the future and a greater awareness of the broad aims of the discipline than it does at present (sitting facing the engine). It should be less concerned with analysis as an end in itself and more with analysis for some specified purpose.

Now since language is the only medium used by theology, and a vital one in sociology (more so than e.g. in physics), an interaction between the two disciplines is going to involve problems of language and vocabulary. I want therefore to look at a problem raised by the word 'theology' if we express it as 'God-talk' and this will lead us to one of the recurring difficulties involved in a meeting of two languages such as those of theology and sociology.

If we consider 'God talk' we can either stress it as *God*-talk or God-*talk*. When we concentrate on the former we are soon confronted by questions of the possibility of such an activity at all, or if it be possible, of the helpfulness or meaningfulness of such talk. Our attention is focussed on the eligibility of matters concerning the inexpressible and the ineffable as subjects for talk, and we find ourselves in what is usually known as philosophical theology. The other stress however, although it is only an emphasis and not an alternative to the first course, directs our attention more to questions of the nature of talk and the properties of words and so to the problem of the nature of God-talk. Now it is of course true that in a sense the whole purpose of linguistic philosophy as it has been developed in recent years is just this, to explore the nature and function of language; but there has been little attempt to explore in detail theological language, as the language used by believing people. In putting the stress on God-*talk* therefore, I am suggesting that the linguistic usage of the religious community be explored, but such an intention at once raises great problems.

It could be taken to mean that the linguistic usage of one community is quite distinct from that of others, so that we may examine each one without reference to a more embracing concept of the proper use of language. It could mean, for example, that religious language can slip through the subtle net woven by careful philosophers simply by saying, 'I do not accept your view of

K

language'. This could then lead to a hopeless linguistic relativism, a break-down of communication between different language systems and an abandonment of the whole idea of 'truth' as being of universal application.

I do not think that all this necessarily follows, but as this is not the chief concern of this paper I can only make a few qualifications and then try to press on. It does seem clear that people inhabit many different language worlds, and it is a matter of ordinary experience that people often do not understand each other because of this. (I would want to stress 'many' and 'often' here, as of course the situation is by no means wholly bleak.) It is also clear that in the sciences and in such fields as history the notion of a 'fact' is far from being a precise one, and this alone must surely give us pause to reconsider the correlative term 'truth'. Finally, I believe that the role of the community in all talk about language is often much too lightly treated, and that it is also of crucial importance in understanding the idea of 'truth' and 'fact'. All these points will appear during the following discussion but must be left for the moment as assertions and presuppositions.

How then are we going to say anything about the relation between theology and sociology? We seem to have given far too much away, for if all languages are even to a degree mutually exclusive then our aim of relating theology to other fields seems simply futile. Perhaps part of the answer lies in seeing that we must not expect to be able to convert the language of one discipline into that of another without remainder, or even to exchange words in any direct way. We must rather be ready to listen for echoes from our own language in another language, or to pick up sympathetic vibrations from apparently unlikely sources. Thus the theologian today may approach the scientist diffidently not only because of doubts about his own subject, but because of his awareness of the possible futility of the approach in any case. He will be encouraged by the fact that theologians from St. Paul to Teilhard de Chardin have poured their insights into a wide variety of linguistic moulds, but in the nature of the case he will have no certainty about the success of his own attempt. With all this in mind, let us look at some non-theological uses of language, and see what they suggest to theology.

ii

One of the most important functions of language is that concerned with problem-solving, and with the closely related task of the conception and execution of courses of action. Two or three examples will show what I mean. There is little to choose between the performances of a rat and a man when faced with a maze, and in some respects young chimpanzees are more resourceful and 'intelligent' than human children of the same age. But as soon as the man can say to himself, 'First right, second left, left again', the rat is left far behind; as soon as the child can name objects and can speak with his parents about the world around him, his world becomes potentially an object-for-him and is immeasurably greater than the chimpanzee's cosmos of immediacy. Or consider my saying to a friend, 'I shall go for a walk in the Parks this afternoon', and carrying out my intention; also Rover sitting before the fire this morning and wandering round the Parks this afternoon. One of the factors which constitutes me a person and Rover not is this very ability to connect events by means of intentions or wishes.

I want to use these examples of illustrate an important distinction between 'actions' and 'events', following the lead of John Macmurray.[1] Both actions and events take place in space-time; that is, they modify the environment and affect the future, for both Rover and I are in the room in the morning and in the Parks in the afternoon, and the Parks are different because of our presence. In the one case, however, it is meaningful to talk about 'purpose' and 'intention' and these are specifiable either in advance or retrospectively, or both; in the case of Rover this cannot be done. My behaviour I shall call an 'action', and that of Rover an 'event', but at once one important qualification ought to be made, for there is a large class of cases where this simple distinction is blurred. Consider the man riding his bicycle to work, or the craftsman fashioning some object. We might ask of both, 'How are you going to do this?' or, 'What have you just done?' and in both cases the point would soon be reached where linguistic descriptions would become impossible, because none had ever been given when the behaviour was first learned. This is the class of skills (and, with modifications, of habits) where the reply, 'I just

[1] Cf. J. Macmurray, *The Self as Agent*, London, 1957, especially pp. 146–164.

know', is the proper one to the question, 'How do you do it?' Perhaps we can regard these as 'activities', being a sub-group of actions rather than of events.

Returning to the basic distinction, it is in social behaviour that the idea of actions is most helpful, and the idea of events most dangerous. To speak of 'the inevitability of events' or 'the tide of events' is to say that a social situation is not properly defined in personal terms; it is to say that purpose, choice, intention have no place in its description, but that it is so because of forces, trends, movements. Now I am not prepared to say that such event language is never appropriate—a naive personalism is so often plainly inadequate as a critical tool—but I would suggest that in the very act of describing a situation in which phrases such as, 'A decided Y', or 'B told C to do X with the result Z' would find a meaningful context, we are using action language. If it makes sense to ask a participant in a situation, 'What are you doing, and why, and how?' then it is possible to conceive of his behaviour as being other than in fact it was (unless the questions and his answers are non-sense) and thus of the situation as being other than in fact it was. It may be possible to describe a situation wholly in event language, but if action language could also or instead be used, but is neglected, then the implications of this neglect, in terms of the denial of the relevance of the personal, should at least be realized.

I want now to make another broad distinction, between what I shall call 'goal language' and 'vision language'. This distinction is central to the argument of the paper, and so I want to treat it in some detail. Goal language is characterized by its immediacy and its precise formulation of problems, while vision language is vaguer and less neat, but is none the less necessary for that. (Is it even always an advantage to replace an indistinct picture by a sharp one? Isn't the indistinct one often exactly what we need?—Wittgenstein.) Goal language is the language of plans and reports, of commands and the steps taken for their execution, of the day-to-day decisions needed to keep a concern or a programme going. It is found on the lips of executives and foremen, of the social worker in the field and the psychiatrist confronted by the patient, of the management consultant or the parish priest at their ordinary business. Vision language has a much more elusive setting-in-life. It is discovered at school in the maxims and attitudes of the teacher, or at university in the early hours of the morning when sublimity and banality mingle with the cigarette smoke and are only, if ever, distinguished in the lives of the adults who later emerge. It is perhaps found in the bath, or listening to Beethoven, or at crises of confidence and conscience, or in rows with colleagues or academic debate. We may say that it provides the (often tacit) background against which goal language is used, but the relationship is rather more complex than that.

Consider the status of goal language without reference to vision language. In a broadcast talk Anatol Rapaport[2] discussed the difficulties involved in introducing a visionary perspective into U.S. foreign policy, where the language of 'hard' science is dominant, and which is 'by definition the sort that deals with well formulated problems, where one knows exactly what one is talking about and has an idea in advance of the nature of the solution'. In this context of talk of fire-power, shipping tonnage, gross national product, public opinion indices and votes, he observes that 'considerations which question the worth of traditional national goals, or which enquire into the quality of life, or attempt to weigh human suffering against the exigencies of global strategy are usually dismissed as vague, sentimental, bizarre or unrealistic'. As another example consider the work of social workers or psychiatrists who do not have at least some idea of what it means for a person to be socially integrated or psychically whole. Without what Dr. Dillistone calls an 'integrating image' the patient or client can only be relieved of the grosser manifestations of his social or psychic disorder, and the wider aspects of his relations to himself, to society or to God must remain unattended for lack of a conceptual vision of wholeness. To give a crude example of this, a man whose work is hindered by persistent headaches may be returned to work by having the headaches treated with pills. If, however, his headaches are found to be related to feelings of frustration at his job, rows with his wife and struggles about religious faith, the pills will still work, but few would argue that the man had been cured or 'made whole'. Perhaps I should say, 'Few in our society today', for in a society in which getting to work is of paramount importance, the vision of man will be that of the worker, and no more. But then such a society would not produce the idea of an 'integrating image'.

[2] In *The Listener* for 26th October, 1967, pp. 527–528.

Finally, a particular difficulty in relating vision to goal language lies in the sheer pressure of immediate problems to be solved, as for example in rapidly expanding and developing urban areas of America, so that Professor Wilbert Moore can reflect on 'the irony that where fundamental research is most important for the long term, it is least possible because of present urgency'.[3]

But if goal language is dependent on vision language for its full perspective, the reverse is equally true, for a vision with no anchoring, actual or potential, in action rapidly becomes fantasy. Now fantasy language may have an important function in the life of a person, keeping him going in dull or difficult situations by offering a picture of other, better times. But it tends to be characterized by the words 'if only' and this leads to two possible relations to action. Either a person's fantasy will be impossible of translation into action, or it will lead to socially unacceptable behaviour, such as the adoption of the persona of James Bond, or the criminal pursuit of the means to realize the fantasy.

The case is rather different with genuine vision language, though we must still ask, 'What is the exact nature of its relation to action?' Jesus's vision of the Kingdom of God was a 'possibility' in that it was consistent with the history and present state of Israel and with the power and promises of God. But how could it be called 'true' or 'real' until it was accepted by a community, however halting or inadequate that acceptance was at first, and without the positive goals which it generated? Unless it had been realized, both in the sense of coming into awareness and of becoming actual, in a community of persons who regarded it as being true, the Kingdom of God would have been no more than one man's dream; and unless it had led to actions in the world, it would have been no more than a corporate dream.[4] When Jesus says, 'If I by the finger of God cast out demons, then the kingdom of God has come upon you' (Lk. 11:20), he is speaking of this embodiment of the Kingdom in action. And when we read how Jesus 'could do no mighty work' in his own village because of the people's unbelief (Mk. 6:1–6), we see the prime importance of the community's acceptance for the coming into being of the Kingdom. At least part of Jesus's agony in Gethsemane was surely due to the

---

[3] In *Uses of Sociology*, eds. P. C. Lazarsfeld, W. H. Sewell and H. L. Wilensky, London, 1968, p. 653.

[4] That is why the distinction between realized and future eschatology is a false one if they are in any sense offered as mutually exclusive.

fear that the vision by which he lived might not be accepted and not change men's lives: men who after all this time could only fall asleep showed few signs of being fired by the vision, and if that did not happen what was the significance of Jesus's life—or death? The vision of the Kingdom did not authenticate itself, and this it has in common with all vision language.

iii

Having established this general distinction, let us look a little more closely at the function of language in providing a verbal framework within which future action may be considered. To conceive of a goal or grasp a vision we must select from the language-stock a form of words appropriate to its expression, but this needs clarification, for what is being expressed is only known in the expression. If I say, 'I have a vision of a better society', but in response to a sympathetic, 'Yes, go on', I am unable to say more, what in fact have I said? To put it another way, if Jesus had never left the wilderness, or if Martin Luther King had never told his people of his dream, could we even speak of their having fantasies? Could we say more than, 'He says he thinks, feels, sees something'? It is a necessary part of visions and goals that they be put into words and communicated to people, and for a man who lives by his vision this is literally a matter of life and death. Thus Jesus's, 'Where two or three are gathered in my name, there am I in the midst', is as much an assurance of his own identity as it is an exhortation to the two or three. He died because his vision was not communicated to the holders of power. This is not to say that a 'flash of insight' may not be received in a pre-verbal form: incoherence, excitement or wonder may all be part of the process, but unless they lead to verbalization it is impossible to talk of visions or goals.

It is clear that our goal and vision language will therefore either use the existing linguistic possibilities of the society in which it is being used, or it will try to create new possibilities and, as it were, carry the society with it. The first course is the more common, though arguably the less significant, and so we must see how what is 'possible' usually depends on the state of the verbal environment at the time.

The term 'semantic field' is used to describe this role of language in ordering our experience and determining the possible conceptual schemes open to us. A simple example would be that of a society's system of colours, or of its kinship system. Thus the Navaho Indians of America have words for our white, red and blue, but not for our black, brown, grey; or again the Malayans have only one word for our 'brother' and 'sister'. More significantly, we may refer to the way in which words such as 'progress' or 'decency' could reflect whole aspects of the underlying beliefs and values of nineteenth century England. But, says Professor Ullmann, 'A semantic field does not merely reflect the ideas, values and outlook of contemporary society, but it crystallizes and perpetuates them; it hands down to the oncoming generation a ready-made analysis of experience through which the world will be viewed until the analysis becomes so palpably inadequate and out of date that the whole field has to be recast'.[5] The implications of this view for both goal and vision language (and for their interconnection) are considerable, and I want to look briefly at three examples from our own time to make this clear.

A confusion of goals may reflect both a lack of vision and a debasement of vision language, so that a regrettable situation may be irreparable because of the destruction of the language capable of putting it right. For example, Peter Winch cites Penelope Hall's book on *The Social Services of Modern England* as stating that it is the duty of a social worker to establish a relationship of friendship with her clients. However, she must never forget that her first duty is to the agency by which she is employed.[6] Here the admittedly vague but certainly potent idea of 'friendship' is lost behind two immediate and incompatible responsibilities, so that the word becomes debased and therefore useless as a means of resolving the confusion. Within such a system a reforming new administrator would be hard put to give the word 'friendship' any clear content, either to the clients or the social workers, though in practice I believe that the social workers' concern for their clients leads to a certain freedom in the interpretation of 'duty to the agency'.

For an example of a semantic field becoming what Ullmann calls 'palpably inadequate and out-of-date' we may turn to some words of Professor Charles Osgood. He writes: 'Scientific control of the environment has already reached the point where we now

---

[5] S. Ullmann, *Semantics*, Oxford, 1962, p. 250.
[6] Cited in P. Winch, *The Idea of a Social Science*, London, 1958, p. 123.

have a new kind of freedom which is positively embarrassing in its richness: freedom to make deserts into gardens, freedom to manipulate our own numbers and even our own genetic make-up, freedom to bring any part of the world to any doorstep by satellite communications. The possibilities are staggering to the imagination, but choice among them demands fresh and apposite propositions about the world.'[7] Yet in such a world, he points out, the language of national independence or of the strategy of the second World War is still used; our ideas of 'balance of power' or 'deterrent value' were developed before the balance could be 'righted' by a nuclear attack; our language about 'commitment', 'freedom', the 'right to self-determination' serves only to resolve a world of complexity to the simplicity of a fairy-story—a fairy-story which we believe.

As a third, more immediate, example we may refer to the previous chapter in this book and consider the nature of the gap between Dr. Klein and her imaginary interlocutor. Both parties are using goal and vision language: for Dr. Klein 'most people live way below their capacity for living' and she 'has a concern for others', and in the light of this sort of vision language she examines a specifiable goal—that of hostels for 'drop-outs' in which short-term sexual liaisons would be tolerated. Her interlocutor, however, is working with much more highly structured vision language in which phrases such as 'marriage is a Christian virtue' and 'man and woman are one flesh' in marriage provide the light which is to be shed upon the problem. But such light is highly selective, and makes the acceptance of mixed hostels simply impossible. It is not just that they would be undesirable or unhelpful, but that there is no place on the semantic map where they could possibly fit, except perhaps as legalized brothels, and so the debate becomes two parallel monologues and soon fades out altogether. Unpacking the reasons for this a little more, we may observe that for the interlocutor the conjunction of the words 'man' and 'woman' in the context of sexual behaviour tends to evoke a fundamental distinction between 'sinful' and 'correct' behaviour, and the latter immediately evokes words like 'marriage', 'maturity' and 'permanence'. These responses are not automatic, and this particular group of words does not exist in isolation from the person's whole vocabulary. Words such as 'sinful' or 'marriage' are used in the

---

[7] In *The Listener*, 19th October, 1967, p. 492.

context of the person's previous experience and of the values, attitudes and actions of his parents, teachers and friends. Also, it could be that in arguing with a less radical person than Dr. Klein, 'sinful' and 'marriage' might be used in a somewhat different way. The usage of the words has been shaped by circumstances, just as it has shaped the course and interpretation of circumstances, but in this particular debate one particular usage is evident, and we may say that this person's whole semantic make-up effectively blocks any attempt to carry on the discussion in other terms. But so of course does Dr. Klein's, and here we must deal with a problem which was implied earlier but which I have left untreated until now.

I have suggested that the way in which we organize our experience and conceive and execute plans for the future depends on the semantic fields which are open before us. I have also suggested that we can either plan in terms of existing semantic possibilities, or change the semantic field to offer new possibilities of thought and therefore of action. But by what criteria do we judge the merits of two or more semantic systems? If both viewpoints in Dr. Klein's paper are to a degree mutually exclusive, how do we judge between them? What content, if any, can we give to the question, 'Is this the right thing to do?' Here, of course, we pick up again the problems which were briefly raised at the beginning of this paper, and by now a little more can be said about them.

Consider first the way in which the word 'judge' occurred in two of our questions above. Professor Stephen Toulmin, in his books *The Place of Reason in Ethics*[8] and *The Uses of Argument*[9] has encouraged us to see the model of the law as being helpful for the examination of ethical problems and for the discussion of logical problems in general. The language of evidence, examination of witnesses, judgement on the basis of evidence and so on, is clearly relevant when we discuss questions such as, 'What ought I to do?', and in this process of judgement the question, 'Why?' will constantly occur, requiring reasons to justify the particular step taken in the argument. But, says Toulmin, there comes a point in the argument where 'moral' reasons, that is, reasons concerning the relation of a proposed action to the interests of others, can no longer be given, either because the succession of

[8] Cambridge, 1950.
[9] Cambridge, 1958.

'Why's' has come to an end, or because two courses of action are equally 'moral' and the grounds for choosing one rather than the other are not reasonable in the sense already indicated. These Toulmin calls 'limit situations', and decisions in these situations are made on the basis of a 'rule of life' or 'personal code', which are reasonable in the sense that they have not developed capriciously, but are unreasonable in the sense that no arguments would serve either to commend or dislodge them, and in that they could not be exhaustively described.

It is, I think, clear that what is regarded as evidence and as a valid mode of reasoning will to a great extent be a function of the philosophical, ethical, legal and cultural traditions of the society in which it is considered, and to this extent our problem remains. The complexities of these relations should make us very wary of any facile notions of what is right and wrong (and, I would want to say, of what is 'true' and 'false'), but the language of 'reasons' and 'evidence' does bridge some of the gulfs facing us. For example, in the argument in Dr. Klein's paper it could be expected that the amount of common ground between the two parties would be sufficient to make the discussion of reasons and evidence in matters relating to the central issue possible and fruitful, and enough could be achieved before the respective 'limit situations' were reached for it to be said that a discussion had taken place. In the same way, an observer of the debate would need a sufficient amount of common ground to enable him to judge between the two positions, though obviously the whole procedure will be characterized by caution, slowness, and sensitivity to the complexities of language which are involved.

The problem is more acute when we confront societies which are wholly alien to the western tradition. An example would be that of a society in which witchcraft was an integral part of the people's belief and practice. In such a society, withcraft would be seen to be compatible with all phenomena, natural and supernatural, so that no evidence or argument would serve to disprove it to the people, no matter how 'scientific' the evidence may be. In such a case, it is difficult to know what it means to 'understand' the society: does it mean to interpret it from a western standpoint, or to attempt to enter sympathetically the world view of the people? It is even more difficult to know how to criticize the society's beliefs, or even to evaluate them and make sound judgements upon them.[10] I believe that such problems, provided by comparative anthropology, throw into relief the difficulties involved in giving 'good reasons' to justify a position one has taken.

So far I have tried to say something of the role of language in the conception and execution of plans, to make a number of basic distinctions and to indicate some of the possibilities and problems of this use of language. I want now to present a brief sketch of a piece of theological linguistic usage before going on, in section 5, to see where the discussion has brought us.

iv

One of the most significant terms which the early church used to express its understanding of the person of Jesus was that of the 'Logos', the Word. Today much of the force of the term has been lost, but it is my contention that in the light of the discussion so far this is a term which might with profit be restored to the theological vocabulary. It is true that the concept of the Word has been very prominent in recent German theology, though with a completely different understanding from that of the approach suggested here. In particular, this usage reflects little of the idea of language as integral to the life of a community, and so cannot link 'the Logos' very closely with the ordinary discourse of men. For my purposes in this section I intend to base my discussion on the use of 'the Logos' in St. John's Gospel, and it is to its meaning here that I now turn.

Recent commentators have stressed the many-faceted nature of the term in the fourth gospel, urging that here, as in much of the rest of the New Testament, it will not do simply to label an idea as either Jewish or Hellenistic: rather does the complexity of the primitive church's world of thought encourage us to see such a term as 'Logos' as being the centre of a cluster of resonances and echoes.[11] In the case of 'Logos' these divide into two groups, based

[10] For two different views of the problem see P. Winch, *The Idea of a Social Science*; 'Understanding a Primitive Society' in *Religion and Understanding*, ed. D. Z. Phillips, Oxford, 1967, pp. 9–42; and A. MacIntyre, 'Is Understanding Religion Compatible with Believing' in *Faith and the Philosophers*, ed. J. Hick, London, 1964, pp. 115–133; also E. Gellner in *Times Literary Supplement*, April 4th, 1968, pp. 347–9. See the subsequent discussion up to May 6th, 1968.

[11] I am aware of the force of Professor James Barr's strictures against making words bear too many 'meanings' from widely disparate sources (e.g. in *Semantics of Biblical Language*, Oxford, 1961, pp. 217–9); but while admitting that a given word has a particular intention in any given passage, I would also want to maintain that in syncretistic communities in particular, and for a writer of the fourth

largely though not entirely on the Jewish-Hellenistic division. In the Old Testament it is important to see clearly the relation between the 'Word of God' and the words used by men. We can see an example of this in the first chapters of Genesis, where Adam is shown naming the animals as they are brought before him (Gen. 2:19, 20). Whether this is 'historical' or not is irrelevant here; what is important is the story-teller's belief that in being allowed to give names to them, Adam—man—was being given authority over the animals. In other words, to name something is to have power over it. The significance of this view is seen in the account of the creation, where the repeated 'and God said' is meant to be not simply a command but an effective claim to lordship. We must also note the direct way in which 'and God said' leads to the coming into being of the sun, moon, seas, etc.

This use of words as powerful and directly effective can be seen throughout the Old Testament, and it provides the background against which the 'Word of God' must be seen. An example will make this clearer:

> For as the rain and the snow came down from heaven, and return not thither but water the earth. . . .
> So shall my word be, that goes forth from my mouth; it shall not return to me empty, but it shall accomplish that which I purpose, and prosper in the thing for which I sent it.
>
> Is. 55:10, 11

Just as a man's words got things done, so did the Word of God, and it was seen as being active in all parts of human life, from the great work of creation to the influencing of prophets and kings.

The other major aspect of the Logos idea in John is drawn from Stoic thought through the mediation of Philo, the Alexandrian exegete and commentator who sought to translate the faith of the Old Testament into the language of Greek philosophy. According to Professor Dodd: 'His (Philo's) Logos is not simply the uttered word or command of God; it is the meaning, plan or purpose of the universe, conceived as transcendent as well as immanent, as the thought of God, formed within the eternal Mind and projected into objectivity.'[12] Whereas for an Old Testament writer God's

---

evangelist's subtlety, the memories of other contexts are a vital part of the word's 'meaning'. As indeed would Barr, as long as it is made clear that 'meaning' does not refer to some metaphysical 'content'.

[12] C. H. Dodd, *The Interpretation of the Fourth Gospel*, Cambridge, 1953, p. 297.

Word would be seen as directly ordering human concerns, for the Stoic this would be too crude, involving the transcendent and unchanging purpose of God too much in the ordinary affairs of men.

Philo's Logos is thus a perspective rather than a creative word: it is the framework within which the dynamic word is uttered, and also the purpose which informs the immediate action. In the succeeding centuries this aspect of the Logos concept was stressed at the expense of the Jewish, and inevitably it became hardened so that what was for John an illuminating image, a flash of light briefly penetrating the mystery, becomes simply an idea to be discussed as an idea among other ideas. What Bishop I. T. Ramsey has called 'the metaphysical telescopes' were brought out, the Logos was precisely located on the metaphysical map, and its inadequacy as a personal category when compared with 'Son' soon led to its decline as a vital force from the theological scene.

But if we attempt to see the Logos in its Johannine sense, that is, as an image potent with echoes, not in a concrete but rather in a symbolic, suggestive fashion, I think we can appreciate a certain symmetry between its two-fold emphasis and the two-fold structure of forward looking language as we have already described it. The Jewish emphasis reflects the character of goal language in its immediacy, its activity and its creativity, while we can pick up our vision language in the broader, more universally purposive categories of the Stoic Logos.

v

Is this parallel anything more than ingenious and mildly interesting? Only if it is seen as what it is intended to be, namely, a very small illustration of the sort of results which might be hoped for if we approach religious language in the way I have attempted. It does not say that John's use of the Logos idea still has value for us *because* it has connections with some modern understanding of language. The fact that such connections can be made tells us virtually nothing about the twentieth century value of the Logos idea: that value will only emerge, if at all, when people consider John's words in the light of such language structures as that used by sociology and find in the text some illumination of their existence, or some broadening of their perspective. A sensitive reader coming to the first chapter of

John's Gospel is bound to have his response to the word 'Logos' influenced by a whole range of overtones, perhaps literary or philosophical or specifically linguistic or simply common-sense, and this quite apart from what he knows of the term's 'real meaning' from commentaries or pulpits. To say, then, that 'the Word' in the context of the behavioural sciences involves idea of planning and action, vision and goal, is to suggest that these usages too might influence a reading of St. John, or at least, contribute to the atmosphere in which 'the Word' is understood. There may well be a case for using, e.g., sociology as a direct instrument for interpreting certain aspects of Christian doctrine in a modern idiom, and Mr. Whiteley's paper is an example of how this might be done. But there is also a case for our maintaining that, e.g., theology has a distinctive approach and language, while being sensitive to the horizons of human experience which other disciplines open up, and to the linguistic possibilities they offer. Thus, when we suggest that there is a certain symmetry between the two-fold emphasis of the Johannine Logos and what we have called goal and vision language, this is not to say, 'For "the Stoic element" read "vision language",' nor is it even to say that the Stoic Logos conception is an analogue of vision language. It is simply to offer one of many ways into an understanding of the Johannine Logos idea by means of a sympathetic juxtaposition of languages.

We come now to the possible relevance of theology for the behavioural sciences, and here for the last time I want to refer to the distinction between goal and vision language. I called vision language elusive and imprecise, providing a framework and a perspective for action, but as we went on, ideas such as 'rule of life', 'limit situation' and even 'semantic field' began to become more or less closely attached to the idea of vision language. These enriched our understanding of it but raised difficult problems concerning the ground on which it might be used, and the way in which its validity might be tested. It seemed to grow out of conflict and introspection and the sheer pressure towards finding a life-style, and the Christian claim would be that in Jesus there is to be found the origin and continuing impetus of such a perspective and life-style. The 'integrating image', the vision of wholeness and the model of human relatedness is to be seen in the life, death and resurrection of Jesus, and this claim is expressed theologically by such words as 'the Word became flesh': from the perspective developed in this paper this would be seen as a claim that the judging, saving activity of God, and the intention of God for the lives of men receive expression in the man Jesus. When we consider his life, the claim would be, we may be brought to a realization of the fundamental purpose of human life, and to the mainspring of action. But this can only be a claim, backed up, to be sure, with good reasons, though never fully explained by them, and this fact is expressed in the words 'became flesh'. That is, the claim the Christian makes is based on a particular human life, a life which was this life and none other, for Jesus was a particular Jew living in a given place at a given time, a member of an occupied nation, implicated in the tragedy of Judas, and so on. It is this man, the words 'became flesh' proclaim, who is the focus of the Christian's vision, and it is this particularity which binds the Christian claim very closely to all visionary perspectives. The assertion of the Christian that his claim is 'really' or 'in fact' the 'true' one because it is founded upon the act of God is simply a part of his claim: it may or may not be the case, but I do not see how it could possibly be decided either way. The Christian visionary claim like all other visionary claims is only given substance in the life of a community and in the actions it generates—actions such as the work of the sociologist.

This, if anything, is what 'the Christian approach to sociology' means: the orientating of the studies and analyses of people in society towards the vision of what is in Jesus. That is, if sociology is to be more 'future orientated', and if sociologists are to sit facing the engine, then in that future, the Christian would claim, the figure of Jesus is to be seen, with his care and compassion, his revolutionary ideas of justice and authority, and his vision of a new society. The actual techniques of the sociologist, as of any specialist, are judged by standards appropriate to the discipline, and at this practical, everyday level there is no such thing as 'a Christian way of doing sociology'. What may be Christian is the vision of what man in society ought to be, or of what society should be, and of this any new theology must speak.

X

LIMITATIONS OF THE SOCIOLOGICAL APPROACH

HENRY COMPTON

'I've never read any books on management', said the Chairman of a prosperous small company which I visited recently. He had built up his own business from a one-man-and-a-boy beginning, and we were talking, in his well-appointed office, about management education.

'It seems to me,' I said, 'that you've got to have what it takes to be a manager. If you haven't got it, books and courses are no substitute for it. But if you have got it, can't the right books and courses help you to profit more fully and quickly from experience?'

'Yes, I think they can,' replied the Chairman, without enthusiasm.

This scrap of conversation epitomises the line of thought that I shall pursue in this paper. I have seen for myself that psychology, sociology and the other human sciences provide serviceable tools for people in responsible positions, but I have come to believe that the existence of these tools increases, rather than diminishes, the need for 'what it takes'; and when I ask myself 'What does it take?' I reach for such old-fashioned words as 'wisdom' and 'character'. The sharper the tools, the more sensitive must be the hands that wield them.

My outlook has been shaped by my limited experience of working in industry and of teaching Communication to managers, trainees, supervisors and workers' representatives. This paper is therefore frankly subjective. It records my personal impression that managers and administrators still rely—and must rely—largely on their personal impressions of the world around them, despite the vast amount of objective knowledge that the human sciences now provide. To say that individual intuitions can give valid insights into reality is not to say that they are completely reliable—experience quickly teaches us that they are not. The crude and costly process of 'learning by experience' is the traditional method of improving the quality of our insights, and I

L

153

doubt whether we shall ever eliminate this process from the hurly-burly of practical affairs. We can, however, turn to science, not as a complete substitute for insight, but as a supplement and corrective, capable of removing some of the error from trial-and-error methods.

My concern in this paper is with all those people who make decisions and issue instructions which affect other people—particularly those who exercise authority in industry and commerce. I will refer to them comprehensively as 'managers'. Among them are the professional managers whose emergence as an influential class was described by Burnham in *The Managerial Revolution*. There are also the foremen, forewomen and other supervisors—one estimate puts the number in the United Kingdom at 300,000—who are in direct charge of workers. There are also national, local and branch officials of trade unions, and shop stewards. All these people work for the most part outside the constitutional system of checks and balances evolved in the political sphere. They make decisions which, in sum, have a tremendous, if incalculable, effect on our personal, family and social lives.

Society needs to know much more about this proliferation of power systems in its midst. The usefulness of scientific studies of this phenomenon is therefore obvious. What I wish to consider here, however, is how much guidance the findings of scientific research can give to people who have willy nilly to make decisions in industry, commerce and administration.

'Making decisions' is a phrase that begs the question of free will. Subjectively, I feel convinced that managers do exercise free will in decision making: the agony of having to choose between alternative courses of action has been a familiar part of my industrial experience, and other people have described their own heart-searchings to me and have asked for my advice. So, basing myself on the intensity of personal experience, I assume that 'decision making' is not just a misleading name for 'conditioned behaviour'. This is of course the assumption that managers make in their daily lives.

If we do have free will, managerial decisions must surely contain an individual element which defies scientific prediction. Many human scientists and management theorists seem to concede this point when they write about 'decision making' and 'problem solving'. On the other hand the frequent use of the words 'behavioural sciences' could imply the belief that we are all automata responding predictably to the stimuli applied to us.

Some scientists seem, then, to be in a muddle about the philosophical aspects of their inquiries. I must, however, leave to philosophers the task of making a philosophical scrutiny of the human sciences. As a practical man I can only note that very deep issues are raised when science turns its searchlight on human affairs; and I shall remain doubtful whether science, as science, can settle these issues. From my standpoint I can make sense of statements about 'human behaviour' if they are taken to be generalisations based on the systematic observation of many people's conduct; but I shall expect to find individual exceptions to each generalization, and for practical purposes I may well regard the exceptions, with their unique, individual character, as more significant than the scientific generalization.

Believing, as they do, that they exercise personal discretion in making decisions, practising managers often say that management is an art as well as a science. This is, for instance, the view taken by Sir Frederick Hooper, in his 'Management Notebook'. Management theorists are, in my experience, less prone to emphasise the artistic element—not surprisingly, since the fine arts are not traditionally academic subjects, although they were evolved in the pre-scientific phases of civilization. In order to put the scientific study of management into perspective, then, we must consider what meaning we can give to 'the art of management'.

Has management anything in common with the fine or the useful arts which would justify us in talking of it as an art? Yes— the painter, the interior decorator and the manager are all doers as well as thinkers. It is true that the manager is mostly concerned with getting other people to do things, and not with doing them himself (so, for that matter, is the architect or the orchestral conductor); this does not alter the fact that the manager's thinking is characteristically untheoretical and directed, like the artist's, towards the activity by which he achieves his goal.

In the second place, the artist and the manager both exercise skills which they have learned through practice. 'Practice' includes a long process of 'having a go' and learning from one's successes and failures. Thus, leading companies usually expect their

trainees to find their feet in real-life situations where the consequences of failure will be serious (though not disastrous). Practice
also includes the imbibing, from teachers and other sources, of a
tradition—the accumulated results of the practice of predecessors
and contemporaries. Even when the artist or the manager rebels
against tradition, it is still an influence on his work. Some of the
most effective managers I have known are gratefully aware of their
indebtedness to the example set by some older manager in their
youth.

In the third place, artists and managers both experience—as I
believe from what I have read and observed—a 'break-through' to
a sense of mastery and achievement. 'To come out on top of the
job' is the popular way of describing this sensation. The awareness
of making prentice efforts fades away. The practitioner finds that
he can 'express himself' in paint, or musical tones—or action. His
practice has led him to practised skill. Nor has he merely mastered
traditional techniques—he has introduced some element of style
that is distinctively his own.

The achievement of mastery in an art (and, for that matter, a
craft) brings an experience of creativity—of having produced
something that previously did not exist. Paradoxically, it also
brings an experience of discovery—of opening up some aspect of
reality that had previously been hidden. This dual experience is,
I believe, known to some managers. It seems to me to support the
claim made by Professor Ian Ramsey in *Biology and Personality*
(Oxford, 1965, p. 185) 'that not only may descriptive events be so
ordered as to disclose a *subject* which while it includes them also
transcends them, but that descriptive events may also be ordered
so as to disclose an *object* which in a similar sort of way transcends
them objectively'.

The experience is, in short, one of 'revelation'. Those who
have reached it seem able to adapt their means to their ends with
effortless ease; they possess and inspire confidence; they transform
their problems by their creative approach.

Mary Parker Follett some forty years ago gave the name of
'integration' to the method of solving problems by creating new
situations. The examples which she gave, reprinted in *Dynamic
Administration*, have become classics of management. A dispute
had arisen, for instance, over an unloading platform for milk
churns, which was situated halfway up a hill. The dairymen who

had to go up the hill were aggrieved because the dairymen who came down the hill always reached the unloading platform first. So Mary Parker Follett suggested a two-sided platform, one side for those who came uphill, and the other for those who came down.

To the list of the common elements in art and management I would add that both the artist and the manager work in some raw material which is in part tractable and in part recalcitrant. The sculptor works in stone, the poet in words—in what does the manager work? The answer—and it is a surprising answer in view of the down-to-earth character that the manager is usually taken to have—is that he works in emotional situations. His raw material is the human psyche.

Of course managers deal with pounds, shillings and pence, with plans and schedules, with buying and selling. All these matters are of emotional concern to people—not necessarily people in the mass, averaged out and generalized, but specific individuals. Tractable in part, recalcitrant in part, human beings are the raw material of the manager's art, which he glosses over or botches at his peril.

Practising managers often express their awareness that human relations are the crucial element in their work, which has been described as 'getting results through people'. It was, I believe, Sir Charles Bartlett of Vauxhall Motors who said that his company had only to be sure of engaging the right people in order to solve all its problems. Supervisors have often told me that their jobs have forced them to be amateur psychologists. 'Jim's got all the know-how to get top output from his machine,' said a foreman. 'Yet we both know he's falling a long way short of what he can easily do. If I can't find out what's making him so bloody-minded, I shall have to sack him. And that won't be a pleasant job.'

The artistic approach, as I have tried to describe it, has parallels with the scientific approach. The artist and the scientist both respect the given facts—the situations which constitute their raw material. Both base their techniques on a traditional accumulation of experience. The scientist framing and testing his hypothesis is engaged in an encounter with his raw materials not unlike the artist's. The scientist, as well as the artist, knows the thrill of discovery.

Nevertheless, there are important differences between the scientific and the artistic approaches to management. The artist's is a subjective method: he is emotionally involved in the situation on which he works. The scientist must try to be objective and detached—to observe without participating. The artist can set to work without any preconceived theories, and he is quite happy to leave unformulated whatever it is that he learns through practice and mastery. Such lessons are perhaps incapable of formulation, at any rate by those who are not artists in words. (Hence, no doubt, the complaints often made by professional teachers of management subjects that practising managers seldom make good teachers.) In contrast with the artist, the scientist has a theory to test, and he is seeking to build up a bigger and better theory—of 'organization' or 'communication' for instance—as a basis for his future efforts.

People with a scientific training doubtless feel that the artist's spontaneous assault upon his raw material is a piece of reckless abandon. Conversely, managers are apt to be suspicious of theories offered for their guidance by scientists who have not experienced personal involvement in managerial work. The misgivings of both must be broken down, so that we can make the best of both worlds.

My purpose now is to question the desirability, or possibility, of an exclusively scientific approach to the practice of management, and to claim that the artistic approach is still valid, and indispensable, despite the advances which the human sciences have made. In defending art I do not wish to attack science, which has clearly become indispensable also, in the complex circumstances of modern life. If I seem unappreciative of science it is probably because I feel that the case for art is in danger of going by default —with consequences that alarm me—if no champions come forward to defend it.

In an endeavour to form a balanced view, let us look at some self-evident benefits conferred by the human sciences and at the same time consider their limitations.

(1) Scientific research gives managers a wider awareness, and a greater range of well-attested information, about the social, psychological and biological aspects of the situations in which they work. It also provides knowledge of situations, outside the manager's experience, from which useful analogies can be drawn. Thus science can draw managers' attention to problems and opportunities that would have gone unnoticed without its aid.

At the same time it can quicken the social conscience by pointing to the far-reaching consequences of managerial decisions. One example of these benefits is managers' growing awareness of the nature of 'groupiness' among workers, thanks to the researches of social scientists.

Over against these benefits, however, we must set the fact that no scientist can uncover the whole truth about the fresh situations which confront the manager every day. This is because each situation is unique and, in part, unprecedented.

A junior industrial manager of my acquaintance periodically receives a telephone call from his 'guv'nor' saying, 'R...'s just gone upstairs to the . . . Department. Run after him quick and see that he doesn't do any harm.' R . . . is the guv'nor's son and has a higher managerial rank than my friend. He is, it seems, a 'difficult' personality—but my friend has learned by experience how to take effective measures when R . . . threatens to cause a strike in the . . . Department. 'After all,' says my friend, 'you have to make allowances for R . . . . He came here from a concentration camp.' It is hard to see how scientific knowledge could equip my friend to deal with his peculiar problem more effectively than he does.

(2) The human sciences provide methods of analysing the human aspects of managerial problems consistently and systematically. They can thus reduce some of the uncertainty surrounding managerial decisions. Well-tried techniques have been developed, for instance, for conducting attitude surveys among a company's employees, and such surveys can supply reliable information about a company's standing in the eyes of its workers; this may correct wishful thinking or superficial impressions.

From the manager's point of view, however, there are two serious limitations to the use of scientific analysis in the human field. First, considerations of time and expense may make it impracticable to hire experts to conduct an analysis, whilst the manager's amateur attempts to be scientific may be no more than well-intentioned bungling. Professor Tom Lupton has suggested in his pamphlet, *Industrial Behaviour and Personnel Management* (Institute of Personnel Management, page 22) that personnel managers will have to become 'technologists of the behavioural sciences' in order to advise top managements on how to produce the best possible combination of commercial efficiency and employee welfare. This is one way in which scientific expertise could find practical application in large organizations, but smaller concerns will hardly be able to afford their own experts, and experts brought in from outside will lack the necessary inside information.

Second, one cannot be sure that all the factors in a managerial situation can be observed and measured by scientific methods—even assuming that the methods of the human sciences are approaching perfection, which seems highly unlikely. A few years ago the head of a large American cosmetics firm commissioned extensive market research to ascertain whether women would welcome red shades of nail varnish. After questioning a representative sample of women the researchers concluded that very few would buy red nail varnish—the majority of those questioned had expressed abhorrence of the very idea. But the cosmetics tycoon had a 'hunch' that red varnish would sell nevertheless. He backed his 'hunch'—with results that we have all seen.

Perhaps those researchers were qualified in the techniques of market research, but not in feminine psychology. If so, we have yet another example of the scientific worker confined to his own compartment and ill-informed about the compartment next door. Perhaps feminine psychology is unfathomable by science. Perhaps there is an unexpected side-light, in this mundane context, on the question whether all parts of the human experience are properly available for scientific investigation—the question raised by Dr. David Lack in *Biology and Personality* (page 46).

(3) The human sciences, like the physical ones, can jerk managers out of mental ruts and make them more enterprising and creative. Thus—to quote from page 5 of the pamphlet, *Human Sciences—Aid to Industry*, published by the Department of Scientific and Industrial Research in 1961—'it seems clear from research findings that the speed at which a man carries out a task depends on the time he takes to decide on what to do and not on the time he spends making the movements. Such work has led to recommendations on ways of reducing the complexity of a task, for example by the use of spatial groupings of instruments and dials, based on the logical flow of tasks, and by colour coding'. A paragraph such as this could turn a manager's thoughts on the organization of work into entirely fresh channels—the creation of which, be it noted, would require considerable artistry in human relations.

Brilliant as are the prospects of innovation opened up by the human sciences, there is a danger that the habit of waiting upon a scientific analysis of one's problems may inhibit adventurous initiatives of the artistic sort. The findings of science are cautious and provisional, and they may sometimes deter managers from acting, as they often have to act, from incomplete knowledge of the situation. The literature of the human sciences abounds with statements that 'much more research is needed' and the temptation is present to defer action until 'much more research' has been completed—research, moreover, which is bound to lag behind the new situations which managerial initiatives create.

The question arises, too, whether all the research undertaken is important enough to justify the money and man-hours devoted to it. Research *can* be a soft option for highly gifted (and less gifted) people who would be more usefully employed in the hard world of manufacturing, buying and selling.

We come now to the subject of courage in management. Research findings are not in themselves a source of courage, although they often point to the need for managers to be courageous. In conversation, managers often comment on the gulf between the cloistered lives of scholars and research workers (as they see them) and the cut-and-thrust of business, with its battle casualties in the shape of stomach ulcers and thromboses. Certainly, the scientist's reputation and career, his prosperity and his family's welfare, are not as a rule so heavily staked on the outcome of his decisions as are those of managers who operate in risk-taking situations (not all managers are thus placed, admittedly). To apply coolly the findings of science may involve long periods of agonizing uncertainty—exhilarating to some temperaments, exhausting to others. This is part of the manager's artistic involvement in his situation. He has to look beyond science for his resources of patience and fortitude.

I do not overlook that scientists also require patience and fortitude to carry on their work. It is, indeed, significant from my point of view that their pursuit of objectivity calls into play personal qualities similar to those exercised by good managers.

Lack of moral courage or 'guts', is a failing often noted by subordinates in their chiefs. A shop steward recently described to me the difficulties caused in his department by the fact that there was only one vernier gauge among forty skilled fitters. 'Jobs are always being held up while we queue for a vernier,' he said. 'We asked the foreman several times to tell the management that we needed more—they're not all that expensive. But every time he told us that the management had refused to buy any more. So at last we went direct to the management, and they told us that the foreman had never asked for more verniers.'

Whilst a foreman may lack the pluck to approach his seniors with a simple request, his seniors may be afraid of communicating with the rank and file. 'Our manager keeps on asking me to explain policy decisions to the men,' another shop steward told me. 'He says that I can do it better than he can. But I always tell him that it's his job, not mine.'

Shop stewards themselves also require moral courage if they are to stand up to the pressures bearing on them from workers and from managements. This may be one reason why, as far as my experience goes, they see clearly the vital importance of 'guts' at all levels in industry. Their conviction stems, not from science, but from their emotional involvement.

(4) As already noted, science offers helpful generalizations based on detailed observations. Professor Lupton in *Industrial Behaviour and Personnel Management* (page 12) contrasts such general notions derived from the findings of systematic research with 'personal notions derived from experience' and he clearly believes that the former are more reliable than the latter. Both kinds of notion, as I see it, have their practical applications, and each kind can complement and correct the other.

One of the practical merits of the scientific generalization is that it may enable a manager to make his orders more acceptable and effective by substituting the impersonal authority of science for the personal 'I'm telling you'. 'Our standard dexterity test shows that this is not a suitable job for you' receives readier assent than 'I doubt whether you're good enough for this job'. It is the de-personalized character of science and technology which enables such specialists as medical officers and methods engineers to exercise their 'functional' authority acceptably within 'line' managers' spheres of command.

Yet once again science simultaneously confers a benefit and creates a pitfall. The continuing growth in the size of many employing organizations, and the spread of automation and computerization, notoriously tend to reduce individuals to the status of numbers on a payroll, to wound self-esteem and constrict personal development. The human sciences themselves call attention to this danger, but in the nature of the case remedies cannot be purely scientific; they must be humanistic and personal.

The complaint is frequently heard among workers that 'we never see the boss'. I have noticed on several occasions that when a company, stimulated by the Industrial Training Act, organizes a course for foremen, talks by 'top brass' give a marked boost to morale; if the course members are allowed to talk freely to their seniors they feel that a new chapter has opened in their lives.

Because of the tensions inherent in boss-subordinate relation-ships a modicum of moral courage is required by higher ranks who seek face-to-face meetings with lower ranks, even in a pleasant atmosphere. Much more courage is required by managers, unless they are strongly sadistic, when they have to have 'a showdown' with a subordinate—when it is a question of, say, dismissal, demotion, reprimand or an unwelcome change in working conditions.

A supervisor of my acquaintance is in charge of a series of two-colour litho offset printing machines. Each machine operator used to do a complete four-colour job in the course of two two-colour 'runs' on his own machine and thus had the satisfaction of seeing the whole thing through from start to finish. The supervisor knew that it would be more efficient to work the machines in pairs, two colours printed on one machine and the remaining two colours on another machine. The idea was unpopular, and the supervisor had to argue his case patiently in conversations with individual workers. The supervisor found this 'very wearing'. But he insisted on carrying out his plan, and he reaped his reward when his men found that the pairing of machines introduced an element of sporting competition which compensated for the lost satis-faction of doing a complete job.

The supervisor knew intuitively that he needed to 'sell' his scheme by man-to-man encounters with individual workers. His methods illustrate the vital part played by the personal touch of the artistic manager. He faced the problem of dealing with unique persons in unique situations, each presenting features which in the nature of the case do not enter into scientific general-izations.

(5) In order to correct my emphasis on generalization in science, I must give due weight to the fact that scientific theories

and laws are derived from the observation of many individual instances. They are based on a far greater range of facts than a single manager could amass. In this way science enables managers to learn lessons from experience wider than their own and to check their impressions against a larger framework of reference. Thus, it has often been assumed, on ideological and emotional grounds, that the more contented workers are the more productive ones, but research has shown that this is by no means always so.

The widened horizon is a great benefit—but again there is an accompanying difficulty. The accumulating literature, even in those younger sciences which have a bearing on management, is so vast as to bewilder the practical man. The D.S.I.R. pamphlet already quoted admits (page 22) that 'a research report is likely to be too long and too littered with technical concepts and language to be thoroughly read by more than the few people in industry who have been trained to think in these terms.'

The managers' problems of seeing the wood for the trees are going to increase as scientific data accumulate, despite the improved methods of information storage and retrieval which scientists are devising for their own purposes. This is only one of the problems created by the tendency for scientific knowledge to be compartmentalized and fragmented as more and more researchers learn more and more about smaller and smaller segments of the total field.

As a non-scientist I do not doubt that scientists experience 'breakthrough' in their own ways, when they hit upon an explanation of hitherto baffling facts. Only the initiated can share the thrill of scientific discovery, however; whereas the artist's or craftsman's 'breakthrough' can be shared by ordinary people.

Far from producing scattered fragments, artists characteristically create unified wholes, however complex the components may be. The details of St. Paul's Cathedral join together in a total impression, which every man in the street can appreciate to some extent. A policy implemented by a master of the art of management has a similar compelling and comprehensible unity, which the rank and file can grasp. The artist's breakthrough is an emergence into a fundamental simplicity, which is somehow greater than the sum of the parts that he organizes. The achievement of such simplicity, with its self-communicating character, is one of the marks of leadership. It has the common touch unattainable by 'technical concepts and language'.

Does the integrated wholeness of artistic intuitions represent some sort of insight into truth? I cannot see how there can be proof that intuitive insights 'speak true', but equally I cannot imagine any proof that they are by their nature illusory. The non-scientist is content with the emotional conviction that when he grapples with his problems they sometimes disclose their inner nature with startling coherence and clarity.

It must now be admitted that the artistic approach, like the scientific, has its limitations. Disclosure by insight, valuable as it is to those who experience it, is fitful and unpredictable and cannot be regarded as being, by itself, an adequate basis for day-to-day decision making. We all know that mistaken intuitions and irrational convictions abound in every walk of life.

Nevertheless, some managers show, over a period of time, that their insights are outstandingly practical and creative. Below their high standard there are many degrees of success and failure. So it seems sensible, since scientific checking can never be complete, to do what is in fact commonly done: to appoint to high positions those who have achieved a lower degree of success.

In every art there are good, bad and indifferent practitioners. We can distinguish one from another only by examining the results that they produce, not by calling for their academic or professional qualifications. Science is more standardised: we know that every duly qualified scientist is at least competent in his specialism, and we have only to consider how far above that level he can rise.

It seems to follow that, whatever light may be shed on the matter by psychology, the selection of managers must remain, like management itself, an art as well as a science. Where the human sciences can be particularly useful is in determining what managers actually do and in what jobs crucial decisions are taken or ought to be taken. Research is being done in both these fields. Meanwhile the examples I have quoted from junior management, from supervision and from the trade-union sphere suggest that much important decision making goes on at lower levels than is customarily supposed. If so, the demand for persons with managerial artistry and moral fibre is one that we shall find it difficult to meet. The ideal state would almost certainly have a greater

proportion of its best people in industry, commerce and administration than is the case in Britain at present.

Managerial decision making has become, in industrialized
societies, one of the main fields open to moral endeavour. No one
with experience of business life would pretend that its moral
tone even approaches the ideal, but the prevailing mediocrity
surely shows how great is the potential for higher achievement.
The first step would be a wider awareness of the moral challenge
of this semi-waste land in our midst—that is largely what this
paper is about.

So far, while gladly acknowledging the scientific element in
decision making, I have suggested that there are also artistic and
moral elements. Now I must go one step further and maintain
that there is—or should be—a religious element. This assertion
stems from my emphasis on the uniqueness of persons and
situations. I have often seemed to discern in some managers the
concern for people as human beings which flows from a religious
conviction of the unique value of every human soul. So in trying
to give a full account of management one ends up by bringing in
categories of thought and feeling which have been expressed
through the centuries in religious language, but which are rarely
mentioned in managers' conversation or in management text-
books.

To talk of 'love of your neighbour' on the shop floor, in an
office or in a board room would be a social error, causing embarrass-
ment to all within earshot. Such is the gulf that now separates
commercial from religious life. Yet spiritual issues are surely
present in the moral dilemmas of managers' working lives. A
recognition of this seems necessary to a rounded conception of the
manager's role in society.

In management and in places of management education one
meets people who believe that everything with which they deal
can eventually be quantified after the fashion of science and
technology. I have opposed this view because quantifications
appear to me to be abstractions from the fullness of reality. I have
stated my own conviction that, taking due account of the abstract
quantifications, we can know reality directly through artistic
insight—to which I would now add that simple outgoing of the
heart which religious people call 'love'.

Paul Tillich has put my point better than I can put it, in *The*

Courage to Be (Fontana edition, page 124): 'There are realms of reality or—more exactly—of abstraction from reality in which the most complete detachment is the adequate cognitive approach. Everything which can be expressed in terms of quantitative measurement has this character. But it is most inadequate to apply the same approach to reality in its infinite concreteness. A self which has become a matter of calculation and management has ceased to be a self. It has become a thing. You must participate in a self in order to know what it is.'

If we are content to regard people as means to managerial or technological ends we shall see no need for a religious approach to management. If we prefer to regard management as a means to human ends, I do not see how we can do without the religious concept of the human soul. Once you become involved in the emotional situations with which managers deal, you find that the religious approach is not starry-eyed idealism, but a tough and practical way of life, based on simple insights which must be tested and applied in unique situations with all the science, artistry and moral courage that you can command.